CONVERGENCE

CONVERGENCE

A Reconciliation of

Judaism and Christianity

in the Life of One Woman

Judith Bruder

DOUBLEDAY

New York   London   Toronto   Sydney   Auckland

PUBLISHED BY DOUBLEDAY

a division of Bantam Doubleday Dell Publishing Group, Inc.
666 Fifth Avenue, New York, New York 10103
DOUBLEDAY and the portrayal of an anchor with a dolphin
are trademarks of Doubleday, a division of
Bantam Doubleday Dell Publishing Group, Inc.

Library of Congress Cataloging-in-Publication Data

Bruder, Judith, 1934–
    Convergence : A reconciliation of Judaism and Christianity in
the life of one woman / Judith Bruder. — 1st ed.
      p. cm.
    1. Bruder, Judith, 1934– . 2. Converts from Judaism—Biography.
I. Title.
BV2623.B78A3   1993
248.2′46′092—dc20
[B]   92-26214
                                            CIP

ISBN 0-385-46874-1
Copyright © 1993 by Judith Bruder
All Rights Reserved
Printed in the United States of America
February 1993
First Edition

DESIGNED BY GLEN M. EDELSTEIN

10 9 8 7 6 5 4 3 2 1

For Frank, because he cares for me
and delights me,
and especially because he can make me laugh

*What would happen if one woman
told the truth about her life?
The world would split open.*

—Muriel Rukeyser

Ash Wednesday

*T*HE PRIEST'S THUMB MADE a deliberate mark, first down, then across my forehead.

Turn away from sin and be converted to the gospel.

What did I feel? First a strangeness. Then a happiness that began as warmth emanating from a tiny point somewhere deep within me, and grew and grew until my whole self was suffused with happiness, all the while I knew, and was pained by the knowledge, that if any of my relatives or forebears were to see me like this, marked with the sign of the cross in ashes on my forehead, they would spit, and cross the street.

How did it happen?

At my wedding, there were three rabbis officiating, and a cantor to sing the blessings.

The first was a distinguished Orthodox rabbi and scholar, my father's first cousin, who called my grandmother Tante.

The second, equally distinguished, was the rabbi of the large suburban conservative temple to which I belonged, of which my parents were prominent members.

The third, then a young man, now as distinguished as the first two, was a Reform rabbi whose wife was my longtime friend, at whose wedding I had been maid of honor, and whose wedding dress I was now wearing.

All that was missing, my husband used to joke, was a Moslem in the wings.

It wouldn't even have occurred to him to mention a priest.

How does such a thing come to be?

I am not speaking to you as one who doubted, or fell away from faith, or who was consumed with self-hatred, or never practiced her faith. It's important to understand that. I was always a devout, observant, believing Jew.

I kept a kosher home for years and years, had *six* sets of dishes, one everyday meat and one everyday dairy, one company meat and one company dairy, one Passover meat and one Passover dairy. Six sets. I read Hebrew, loved the language and the songs and the stories, observed the holidays, could conduct a seder, believed in God in an unquestioning sort of way, was proud to be part of his special people, his chosen people. My daughter and son were bar and bat mitzvahed. I was a trustee of my temple, the author of a "Jewish" book who lectured to Jewish audiences, and my husband and I were regulars at Friday evening services. I led a full and busy Jewish life.

What happened?

When I told my sister Mindy that I had become a Roman Catholic, she sat still for a moment, then blurted out, That's the craziest thing I ever heard of!

Well, Mindy, I think it's the craziest thing I ever heard of, too.

But if there's one thing I've learned about God, it's that he often asks of us crazy things.

And painful things.

St. Teresa of Avila, an outspoken lady, once upbraided God.

If that's how you treat your friends, Lord, she said, it's no wonder you have so few!

And yet eventually, if one perseveres long enough, one discovers that God's nonsense is wiser than the world's wisdom.

Or so I believe.

One icy night my husband and I skidded and did a 180 degree turn on the Long Island Expressway.

I never want to do *that* again.

There is a widespread belief that a conversion involves such a radical turn, a 180-degree skid, an overturning of one's whole life, so that one ends up, as we did on the expressway, facing the opposite way from where one began.

Not so.

I did not run off to an ashram or a monastery. I did not get a divorce.

I live the same life I always did, have the same husband, children, house, telephone number, zip code. The same face.

The shift in my perspective has been small. Two degrees, perhaps, five degrees at most. But that was enough. The "greenhouse" effect that scientists predict will drown the shorelines of the world and alter its food patterns and habitations, in short, will transform the earth, depends upon a rise in temperature of only two degrees Farenheit.

And so, the slight shift in perspective that this story tells about has been sufficient to transform my life. Within the contours of the old landscape, without anything much being discarded, all has been made new.

Within my old life, I lead a new one.

I said that little was discarded in the fashioning of this new life. Perhaps it is more accurate to say that I *exchanged* a few things—Friday night services for morning Mass, the bima for the sanctuary, a congregation for a parish. I can play Catholic geography (based on parishes) as well as Jewish geography (based on relatives). I was a reader before, now I am a lector. My experiences as a Roman Catholic have been much the same as my experiences in Judaism, because I am one and the same being. So, too, the symbols by means of which I live my life with God reflect a single Reality. Light is light, and divine, whether it is the sanctuary lamp or the vigil light at the tabernacle. For that matter, a tabernacle is a tabernacle, and God is present equally in Torah scroll and consecrated wafer. I see these things as in a stereopticon: two diverse images merge in the brain to become one fuller, more dimensional picture, and so my worship is both familiar and new.

What happened to me is generally described as a conversion. But conversion is a painful word. So painful was this experience for me, so terrible the sense of apostasy, of my traitorousness toward my whole life and people, that it threatened to keep me from doing that which at the same time I longed ardently to do, to become, which did not feel to me like apostasy at all, but like some natural process which simply happened to be incomprehensible.

When the pain was at its height, a new friend, a very wise monk of a unique religious order, suggested to me that, if conversion were so painful a concept, why did I not think instead in terms of *convergence?* In me, two things ordinarily thought of as incompatible were meeting. The stereopticon effect, after all, is a kind of convergence, and that was how I was experiencing what was happening to me.

That helped.

If conversion is a painful word for you, then you can translate this experience as an awakening, or a turning, or an illumination, a passage from one tradition to another, whatever evokes in you the least discomfort. But for me, this is a convergence story.

This is only a small-scale epic, a journey from one side of a door across a threshold to another. It is not about Judaism, nor a critique of it. Judaism was the way, the metaphor, the image of childhood for me, the backdrop of my whole growing-up life; so my relationship with Judaism is a major part of my relationship with my own history. This story is not about Judaism, it is about me.

I came to the end of a long childhood lived in emotional and psychological dependency. When I lived so many years as a child without knowing it, I lived *seriously,* anxiously, worrying, weighed down by responsibilities real and imagined, lived in the illusion of being able, God-like, to do everything, especially to run my children's lives and protect them from the dangers of this world.

Now that I have, at long last, "grown up," I am more childlike, lighthearted, eager, ready to meet the new. At least at my best I am.

I live joyfully, or try to.

(Not always happily: only fools live in paradise on earth.)

To live joyfully is to live in hope.

And I seek—not always, but at my best and strongest—not illusion or comfort or protection, but truth.

Leaving home has been for me a journey of a single step. But that single step was almost insurmountable. In my stubbornness and balkiness and deep-rooted fears, I put God to a lot of trouble. But in the end God prevailed.

Thank God.

This, then, is the story of a little journey through space and time and memory. But before I begin, I want to make one thing very clear.

I believe that God has worked with me and within me to heal old wounds and make the crooked straight in just the way in which I needed it.

I do not believe God wants Jews to become Christians.

It is a sin against the Holy Spirit and God's infinite variety to believe such a thing.

Rarely does God call for something so radical, or scandalous. If I had been open to God's will in any other way, I'm sure God would not have asked it of me, either.

But I was not, and so this was the way my story had to be.

I keep saying *my story,* but it isn't, of course. It's *God's* story, the activity of God in my life, which I observe and recount in awe and humility, detached by grace, because it felt like a miracle to see God shaping my life so clearly. Sometimes it still does.

I believe that God is always working in *everyone's* life. It is simply that, except perhaps for saints and maybe even for them, we are, in the ordinary, everyday way of things, unaware of God's activity in us. Generally it is only in the sudden jolts, those unexpected, uncomfortable, even terrible moments of grace, that we become vividly aware of God moving and shaping us.

This is such a story, and it began—

My first Ash Wednesday was in 1983, but my story begins long, long before that, in Brooklyn, in Beth Israel Hospital, on Election Day, 1934, the day I was born.

Or maybe before.

Mysteries, of Several Kinds

HE BRIDE CAME, A MOURNER, to her wedding. There was no music in the Lower East Side hall that day, and no dancing, and if the date had not been set already, there would perhaps have been no wedding.

Perhaps no me.

It was probably on that very wedding night that I was conceived, from the sperm of a man not long ago jilted, joining an egg in the womb of a woman in mourning for the death of her father within the previous year.

Ritual Jewish observance prescribes full mourning for seven days, somewhat modified for thirty, and eased, but still observed, for eleven months more.

But my mother mourned, I think, for the rest of her life.

Oh, not outwardly.

She was good-looking, in company vivacious and lively. She sang. She danced. But something was missing at the heart. Passion, I guess that's what was missing, the fuel of love and relationship. If there had ever been passion before, it had died away by the time she married, or shortly afterward, and there was little left to warm her husband or her two older daughters. I suspect that there had one day been passion, because she was capable of it. It kindled, or rekindled, twelve years later with the birth of her third daughter, then burned so fiercely that it threatened to consume its object, the too-well-beloved. But for my father and me, and for my first sister, born four years later, we were acquainted with a mysterious, chilly lady in mourning who kept her own secrets, locked them deep away somewhere, never permitting us to glimpse them, nor had she time or patience to look upon our feelings. A mystery lady of sudden actions and angers who, I now think, embodies for me Winston Churchill's description of Russia, "a riddle wrapped in a mystery inside an enigma." My own Mother Russia. Might her personality have been a heritage brought by my grandparents over the ocean from Bialystok to Beaumont? She was planted in, and sprung from, Texas soil, but she was surely a Russian seed, my mother.

Whatever her secrets were, she took them with her to the grave. We never knew them, my first sister and I; and we never really knew her, this being with whom we lived intimately all the years of our growing up, nursed at her breast, and tended by her hands.

My mother's hands—

Instead of memories, of which I have very few, I have photographs.

Judy's mommy.

Bashful.

Whatsah mattah, honeh.

What the photographs show: an anxious baby, forehead furrowed, awkwardly posed, frowning.

There I am, see, that lumpy bundle, held gingerly at arm's length; and again, perched stiffly on her knee, her arm bracing my back. But her fingers don't curve to hold the baby. They rest straight and out-stretched on her knee.

My mother's hands.

She could do anything with those hands. Big hands, nicely shaped, strongly knuckled. She could roll stuffed cabbage and press and stamp and slice all kinds of cookies, and knead bread, and braid challah; and she could sew and knit and crochet, and wash clothes and iron, and carve rough little figures out of Ivory soap. She could trim roses and make poultices and clothespin dolls, shuffle cards for solitaire, use rectal thermometers, slap, give enemas.

And so much more! In photographs and yearbooks and newspaper clippings, all lost now, we saw with our own eyes, plain in faded black and white, she could rein in a horse, throw a discus, put the shot, play the violin, tambourine, and castanets. There wasn't *anything* she couldn't do with those big, competent hands.

Except, perhaps, to cuddle a firstborn. To hold a baby close and safe. To mother me.

I remember my mother's hands dragging snarls out of tangled hair before braiding it, swiftly ripping off Band-Aids, making cream cheese and jelly sandwiches, telling card fortunes, and smacking a defiant or nagging or whining child.

Busy hands. Always doing useful things.

A year or so before her death, we brought my mother to a cousin's country home for their daughter's bat mitzvah party. She was so frail and unsteady that she had a hard time negotiating the flagstones up to the front door; the flight of steps down to the basement for cocktails was impossible. Even the living room, where chairs were crammed around crowded tables for the festive dinner, was too much for her, too crowded, too noisy, too *much*.

So she sat in the study on a sofa, while her daughters and her sons-in-law and grandchildren took turns bringing food and sitting with her. She sat quietly and heavily, leaning awkwardly on the sofa, a little off balance because of a degree of Parkinson's. Most of the time she sat with her hands in her lap, idle, lying flaccid, except when, intermittently, her right hand trembled with that tremor of old age. And when she was a little agitated or overstimulated, that quiescent figure with quiescent hands, the tremor in her right hand became stronger and stronger, her right hand rolling fiercely in her lap like a rudderless boat caught out in stormy seas.

My mother's hands.

My father holds me tighter, closer. I beam when he is taking the pictures. I was in love with him. I was going to marry him. We pledged our bond with cigar-band rings. Here we are, on my fourth birthday, kissing. The golden days, two months before he betrayed me, before my sister was born.

Betrayal.

My parents knew one another for a sum total of perhaps four weeks spaced out over four years, when my mother came from her home town of Beaumont, Texas, on an annual buying trip for her father's store, and she met and was courted by my New York father, a newly qualified and struggling lawyer.

They were handsome creatures, both of them, tall, well-dressed, well set up, black-haired, strong-featured. Her eyes were dark, she was tan, they cast her as a "high-yaller" in a body-molding sequin dress in some Little Theater performance back in Beaumont; and she danced the Charleston and the Black Bottom with verve, dark eyes flashing. She played the violin on public tour. My father sometimes called her *Orche Tchornia,* Russian for "Dark Eyes." And he, he was dashing, too: green eyes and a quick mind, a ready wit, a smooth tongue; he was a good talker, a lawyer, a professional man. A New Yorker.

What did they see when they looked at one another? What expectations, what projections, what dreams and desires did they bring to their wedding day? How do you superimpose the crowded tenements of the Lower East Side on the wide-open spaces of the Lone Star State? Juxtapose rusty fire escapes and wisteria-hung verandahs? He went to the beach at Riis Park or Coney Island on the subway, she rode to the local swimming hole on the back of a horse, for God's sake! How exotic she must have seemed to him; what urbane strength he must have offered her.

And what bitter disappointments they must have found. Within months the quarrels had begun, lifelong quarrels, the tempers, the misunderstandings.

I remember the sounds of quarreling, and the louder sound of not-speaking. What I don't remember are any sounds of tenderness, nor do I remember seeing any tokens of it between them, not kissing nor caressing nor stroking—

Perhaps they did, behind closed doors.

If so, they kept those mysteries strictly private. Not in front of the *kinder*, they whispered.

The sounds of anger, though, they were permissible.

Sad, so sad.

My mother's face lit up when she talked about her father. Then, and only then, her voice was tender. Wistful.

"He was the handsomest man."

I knew he was dead. That was all I knew about my grandfather Max when I was a child, that he was the handsomest man. And dead.

Death was alluded to only in whispers at our house. Suicide was a word that was taboo.

When, then, did I first begin to piece together the story of my grandfather's death? It took years to form a coherent narrative, and I offer it now with no firm conviction that this is, in fact, the truth of what happened. Archaeologists reconstruct lost civilizations on the basis of a few bones, a handful of potsherds, and conjecture. The civilization in question being, fortunately, vanished, they have little to fear by way of contradiction. But who knows if in truth ancient Sumeria or Crete bore the slightest resemblance to what we accept now as authoritative fact? And as for the life that was lived in those places, how do we even begin to know the truth of it? For that matter, maybe dinosaurs looked not in the least the way they do in the Museum of Natural History, or Walt Disney movies. It was people who put together those bones, not the dinosaurs themselves whose flesh and spirit once animated them.

So, with that disclaimer, I offer this child's archaeology of my grandfather's death, which begins, not with him, but with his oldest son, my uncle Sam. To keep him from playing around with *shiksas* in the store while his father and mother went out of town on extended business, Sam was married off to a first cousin imported from the East Coast. A pretty, fluttery little pouter pigeon of a thing, a good-hearted, but hardly quick-witted young woman who swiftly bore him two sons, neither of whom was *quite right*. Sam, the ladies' man.

He had the bluest eyes, my mother said. And the longest eyelashes. They curled all the way back to his eyebrows, my mother said, marveling.

The handsomest son of the handsomest father.

Sam worked in my grandfather's prosperous dry goods store. In 1929, though, my grandfather lost his savings in the stock market crash; gradually people could no longer afford to shop in the store, so business was bad. People could shop, actually, but they couldn't afford to pay, except by barter. But my grandfather couldn't pay for *his* merchandise with chickens or butter. Times were hard.

And some time, no one knew exactly when, my uncle Sam took out an insurance policy. And a little while after *that,* he swallowed cyanide.

Remember the e. e. cummings poem that ends:

> and what i want to know is
> how do you like your blueeyed boy
> Mister Death

It makes me think of my uncle Sam.

He left a note saying his father could use the insurance money to save the store.

Because, you see, that's who he'd named as beneficiary. His father. Not his plump little hen of a wife, or his two sons who had something (unspecified) wrong with them. His father, who'd married him off at eighteen into this destiny, to keep him out of trouble.

At the funeral, they had to hold my grandmother Ida back from jumping into the grave. My grandfather never recovered, so they said.

One day in 1933 my grandfather didn't come home. After a search, his body was found down in the railroad yard, mangled by a train, in the railroad yard where he had no call to be. Did he fall? Or did he— *ssh.*

Only whispers.

And I didn't hear even the whispers until I was a young woman. Before that there was only a veil of silence and mystery over my grandfather and my uncle Sam, the handsomest men. Vanished heroes.

I only know one other story about my grandfather.

It was when his youngest son was desperately ill, and the whole family was anxiously keeping vigil at the hospital. As my mother told it, her mother, my grandmother Ida, was no help in this crisis, she was too emotional, and carrying on, and anyway, someone had to take all the other children home. And so my grandfather turned to *her,* turned past his wife to his eldest daughter, and said, Everyone can go home and Libby will stay here. I can depend on Libby.

She repeated that solemnly, like a presidential citation: I can depend on Libby.

Her pride. Her burden.

And then—

Betrayal.

Accidentally? It had to be accidental. Because if it were *on purpose*— Unthinkable. Push away the thoughts, press on the lid.

And yet the mystery remained for her, the mystery which was my grandfather's life and death, and which he took with him to his grave, as my mother kept her secrets and took them with her, to hers.

So that was the way things stood at the moment of my conception, and my coming to term, and at my birth.

I was named, in English, Judith Elaine. But my Hebrew name is Esther Leah, after two queens, one my paternal great-grandmother, my grandmother's mother, an East Side grande dame, strong willed, imperious, domineering. And after the great Jewish heroine, Queen Esther, first a favorite concubine of the Persian king Ahasuerus, then his consort. She saved her people by her beauty and her bravery; and when I was young I burned to do the same, to grow up to be a heroine. God knows there were enough people in my family alone who needed saving.

At the same time, though, my birth was, religiously, quite ordinary

and unceremonious. There were no sacred mysteries necessary to sur-
round it, no *brith,* ritual circumcision; no *pidyon ha-ben,* redemption of
the firstborn. Those weren't for daughters. Only for sons. Sons are
circumcised, sons are redeemed.

I was a girl.

I was just born.

Mostly About Grandmothers

M Y MATERNAL GRANDFATHER WAS DEAD before I was born.
I did have a paternal grandfather, at least for a while. He dressed always in black, and had a long white beard, like a prophet, and sometimes he would offer to take me and my sister on his lap as he sat in his kitchen in his black rocking chair, and then he would magically discover from his cloud of white beard a penny for each of us.

A penny was a lot of money in those days. It would buy a fistful of candy from the little store across the street. But even for a whole penny, we were usually reluctant to climb into his lap, the two of us, my sister and I. He seemed so stern. Awe-inspiring. Scary.

And later, when we might have changed our minds, he no longer had a lap for us, no longer rocked in the black rocking chair, but lay all day long, I suppose all night, too, on the narrow bed in the tiny dark front room with its blinds always drawn, lay there quietly as prostatic cancer gnawed its way throughout his body until he died.

Then it was my grandmother who inherited the black rocking

chair, but she never invited us up into her lap. She rarely sat in the rocking chair anyway, at least not when we came visiting. She bustled around the kitchen, and when she sat down, sat with her visiting grown-up children and older grandchildren at the large, round oil-cloth-covered table that took up half of the big room. No one else seemed to be allowed to sit in her rocking chair, though, not even Uncle Shu, who lived with her in the old brownstone on Keap Street in Williamsburgh, Brooklyn. Mostly it stood empty, the rocking chair. Yet we were allowed to use it, my sister and I, separately and together, to sit in its spacious hard wooden lap, and rock and rock, while the grown-ups around the table vigorously discussed and argued matters that we probably wouldn't have been interested in anyway, and as the discussions and arguments were always in Yiddish, we couldn't in any case begin to understand them. My grandmother had already been a grown young woman with a couple of children before she came to America, and she never learned enough English to carry on a conversation. She lived to be ninety-six years old, and for a large part of my life I visited her almost every Sunday, and never once was I able to talk to her.

I didn't care so much when I was young.

My mother claimed that from the very beginning, when I was just an infant in arms, I hated to go to my grandmother's house.

You almost seemed to *know,* she'd say, in a curious, satisfied kind of voice, and you'd start to cry when we got into the car.

It was often boring, it's true, at my grandmother's house, with people speaking a strange, alien language, and it could even be scary, when my grandfather lay silent and dying in the next room. But it had its attractions. Like my grandmother's shiny black sewing machine powered by a foot treadle, which we played with. And the newspaper squares that were cheaper than store-bought toilet paper. And the big oilcloth-covered table made a satisfactory cave to crawl under, to sit and watch the grown-ups' legs and feet.

We never ate a meal at my grandmother's house. I realize this for the first time, with a shock: she was poor. But she would give us cold water to drink in strange-shaped glasses. When I was older, I learned that those glasses had held *Yahrzeit* memorial candles, candles burned each year to honor the anniversary of family deaths; and then I didn't want to use those glasses anymore. Drinking from dead mouths, ugh. But before that I enjoyed the water, which accompanied my grandmother's flat, dry, hard onion cookies. They were as pale and dusty as cardboard, but I loved their diamond shapes and faint onion aroma and taste. She gave us raisins, too, not black and crinkled, like at home. Golden raisins these were, plump and sweet. And there would be peanuts in their shells. My father loved peanuts, and the empty shells would pile up in front of him on the oilcloth. He taught us how to pinch the shells to crack them and release the nuts, and then to rub off their russet skins, and split the nut very carefully with our fingernail to reveal the little bearded rabbi hiding inside each peanut. If you don't believe there are rabbis in peanuts, then try it for yourself. But you have to be very careful when you separate the two halves, or you'll crush the poor little rabbi, or at least break off his beard.

She was small, my grandmother, and dry and wrinkled, not unlike a raisin herself, but fierce, her eyes hooded and her nose beaked like a bird of prey, with shiny elaborate bright brown hair, strangely youthful around her deeply wrinkled face. It was years before I realized that the bright brown hair was not her own, was actually a *sheytl,* the wig worn by Orthodox Jewish married women to cover their cropped heads, for much the same intention that nuns used to wear wimples. Wig or wimple, little difference which one is hidden in.

My grandmother was always little and bony and wrinkled, and when I was young I already thought she was old, so as I grew and aged it was perhaps not so remarkable that to me my grandmother never aged, but looked the same, almost until she died.

Hannah Toba.

How well could I have known her, this daughter of Esther Leah, the matriarch for whom I was named? Not very well, I suppose. We had little, not even a language, in common. And yet, when I was much older, and a mother myself, I felt an odd closeness to her, and when she died, an unexpected grief and sense of loss. Now, too late, I wish I could have talked with her, my little, fierce, wrinkled grand-mother. We might have discovered that, after all, we did speak the same language.

Her nephew, a noted rabbi and scholar, gave the eulogy at her funeral. It was a wonderful eulogy. She was a second mother to him, he said. A loving aunt to all the Lower East Side when he, like my father, was a little boy. I hadn't seen this nephew, my cousin, for years, not since he had been one of the three to officiate at my wedding. But I admired and respected his scholarly achievements, and I was moved and grateful for what he had said about my grandmother. So, as we were waiting for the cars that would take the mourners to the ceme-tery, I went over to greet him, and to thank him. I knew better than to try and kiss or hug him, my first cousin once removed, because he was Orthodox. Instead, I offered him my hand.

And immediately he stepped away from me, put both his hands behind his back and said quietly, unemotionally, I don't shake hands with women.

So there are some random scenes to remember my grandmother by: the brownstone on Keap Street, the oilcloth-covered table, the rocking chair, the sewing machine, my grandmother's *sheytl,* the yellow raisins, and my cousin's hands behind his back outside the funeral home in Bensonhurst on the day after my grandmother died.

My *other* grandmother, my mother's mother, looked a lot more like grandmothers are supposed to: plump-cheeked, plump-bodied, white hair drawn back in a bun, dressed, in my memory, in a housedress and apron. Motherly looking.

But I don't remember her as motherly at all. Despite the soft plumpness, the apron, she didn't cuddle or hug. No laps available for sitting here, either. Nor did she smile much. Life was serious business.

My paternal grandparents had come from Sienawer, a little town then in Austria-Hungary, but now, if it still exists, in Poland, near the Russian border. Not that Sienawer ever actually moved from where it was. The events of the world moved, overran it, and all the Jews who'd stayed behind there, unwilling or unable to do as my grandparents had done, leave their homes and seek their fortune elsewhere, are dead long since in the Holocaust. My grandfather found no great fortune in the new country. He peddled silks from a pushcart on the Lower East Side until, at the time of his death, he had a tiny store, a hole-in-the-wall kind of place really, but his. And his children grew up to be 100-percent Americans.

My maternal grandfather, Max, the one whose life ended in a train yard in Beaumont, Texas, had begun it in Bialystok, in Russia. His older brother had fled from conscription in the Tsar's army, sailed to Mexico, and from there crossed the border into the United States at El Paso, where he stayed and settled. My grandfather, already married, but poor, and with no prospects, followed him a few years later, landing at Ellis Island en route to Chicago, and a job with a cousin. But that didn't work out, so he too set out for Texas. He went, not to El Paso, but to Beaumont, which I interpreted as meaning that he and his older brother can't have been very close, because usually immigrant siblings helped out one another. At any rate, my grandfather got a job in Beaumont, and eventually sent for his wife, and worked very hard, and at last became the proprietor of a prosperous dry goods store. But before that, there were plenty of lean years for them in this still rough and rugged Southwestern town of Beaumont, and my mother would tell us stories about her mother driving a buggy into town over dirt roads, and milking cows and churning butter.

Texas!

It was a land as fascinating and fabulous as Sienawer, and even better, because we actually got to go there, not once, but many times. For years, beginning when I was two, every other summer my mother and I, and then my sister as well, would depart by train for a six weeks' visit in El Paso. Never to Beaumont; there was no close family left in Beaumont any more. The store's failure and my grandfather's death took place before I was born, and soon my uncles and aunts had migrated to El Paso, where my great-uncle's branch of the family was flourishing, my great-uncle who ran away from the Tsar's army (or so the legend went) and went to Mexico and then walked all the way across the border to El Paso, where he'd become a junk man, then a scrap dealer, scrap metals, a steel mill: he never looked back. Which proves, I suppose, the superiority of junk as a commodity over those found in retail stores.

When we came to El Paso for our summer-long visits, it was at my uncle's house that we stayed, my mother's youngest brother, the one who'd been so sick in the hospital. He was away working all day long, though; and was a remote figure to me when he came home, anyway, with his pale eyes, and pearl gray Stetson hat, and West Texas drawl, nothing like my own father far away in Brooklyn, whom I missed too much to bear thinking about. So in my mind El Paso means a house full of women, my aunt, my three girl cousins, my mother, my sister, and me.

And my maternal grandmother, of the oil fields, and the cows and chickens and horse and buggies?

Most of the time I was a young girl, she lived in Brooklyn, and so it wasn't in Texas at all, but in an apartment house in Flatbush that we visited her in my growing-up years, and I have no fond memories of those visits. In fact, I have hardly any memories of them at all. That grandmother, my grandmother Ida, spoke English. But I don't re-member any conversations with her any more than with my other grandmother. We both spoke English. But we still didn't speak the same language.

So who, if anyone, did speak my language, in Williamsburgh or in Texas?

Not my cousins, not really, even though I liked and admired them with my whole heart. My Texas cousins, Joan and Mimi, wore jodh-purs and western boots from Tony Lama when they went horseback riding.

Horseback riding!

I, who would have given my soul for my own boots from Tony Lama, was afraid of horses, and after once going around a ring on the back of one of those powerful and unpredictable animals, chose to stay at the side of the corral instead, watching my cousins ride, and wishing we would go home soon.

Clearly, this was a country for strong people, and for brave ones. Where I came from, nature was small and domestic.

I was a city child. I walked on paved streets, paved sidewalks, paved alleyways. I was never aware of walking on the earth. We had no fields, no crops, no rivers, no lakes, no mountains or woods. Even at Coney Island, at the beach, we rarely went out onto the sand up to the ocean, but walked, fully dressed, along the boardwalk and frequented the children's rides.

My rivers were the waters rushing in the gutters after a hard rain; my mountains, the mounds of snow my father shoveled in the back. Wildlife in Brooklyn consisted of Japanese beetles and mosquitoes and little black ants on the front stoop with which my sister Mindy would play; and inside the house there were silverfish. Not roaches, which are ugly and come from dirt, but translucent darting silverfish, which feed on books and glue and papers, a civilized diet.

And here was I transported to a land of bats and scorpions and Gila monsters and horses, a fierce land for fearless people like my jodhpured, booted cousins, who could ride and run barefoot on permanently calloused feet and seemed to fear nothing, while I was afraid of whole lots of things; and who called everybody "y'all" and said the word *water* in a way that was different from my way, so that theirs sounds more like *wawder*, and they teased me about my N'Yawk accent, and made me say *wah-ter* again and again, and they'd laugh.

They were the ones who had the funny accent, but this was their country, and I couldn't tell them so. Small, skinny, in awe of my big, accomplished, vigorous, self-confident cousins, I was often homesick. As August waned, I was glad enough to board the train for Brooklyn. But something, all unknown, came with me.

Something that did speak my language.

It wasn't a Who, exactly. It was more a What.

El Paso del Norte is just what its name says it is, a pass in the desert between mountain ranges. Wherever you are, if you lift up your eyes, you encounter the hills, foothill mountains they are, the Franklin Mountains. Now I'd never read the Psalms. I didn't know the Psalmist's promise of help from the hills. It was subliminal, that's all, the comfort I got from the sense of presence, from the great images, the archetypes, a desert that spread until it bumped up against bare-sloped jagged purple mountains far away, mountains that pierced the vast blue Texas sky, the biggest sky, the highest mountains, the broadest desert I had ever seen, or could imagine, a *natural* kingdom without limit or boundaries that belonged, not to fathers or mothers, nor to grandfathers or grandmothers, but to Someone, or Something, that was Other, that spoke to me in a language without words. A language beyond words, so that I couldn't know the full meaning of this landscape, this desert, these mountains until 1978, when I had completed a draft of my first novel, *Going to Jerusalem,* and my husband and I were touring Israel, to pick up geographical atmosphere for the final draft.

We had driven out from Jerusalem early one morning, going to the Dead Sea and to Masada. The van jounced on its way through the Judean wilderness, and then I was there in a brown and stony desert, with

hills folded like lions' paws stretching almost to the road, bare and brown like the Wild West of America, but instead of sagebrush and the tumbleweed of the West were here terebinth and saltbush. And then those folded hills were replaced by higher, sterner mountains, crags of sandstone . . . and above us arched a vast, deep blue sky, truly the vault of heaven, and something inside me leaped toward the arid land and whispered, "I come from this desert."

Oh!
I come from this desert.
This was no strange country, then, but my own.
These were my hills of home.
The palms at En-gedi, the palms of El Paso.

The desert, the mountains, the mountains of El Paso, alien, and home.

I speculate about it: the Franklin Mountains; I married Franklin, his brother Mel moved to El Paso long before I ever knew of Frank; my young cousin Albert and Frank's nephew Ken grew up as best friends; my someday-to-be brother-in-law's second wife was the sister of my cousin Joan's husband's first cousin—

What a tangle of families!

And there were Frank and I, living our separate lives, not even knowing of one another's existence until I was well in my twenties and Frank past thirty; and here were our parallel lives converging all the time, converging two thousand miles away from New York, in El Paso, in the shelter of the Franklin Mountains.

Unlike my mother and father who, rather than converging parallels, proved to be more like oil and water, the oil of the fields around Beaumont, where my mother grew up, and Brooklyn water, or wah-ter, that Easterners and Westerners disagree on how to pronounce. My parents' wedding of East and West crossed other, less visible lines than color or religion or nationality; theirs was a mixed marriage, oil and water.

And oil and water do not, cannot, mix.

God of Light

OWARD THE END OF SUMMER, 1938, we moved from our apartment in Flatbush into a house in Sheepshead Bay that had no history. It, and much of its neighborhood, was brand new, carved out of a sandy waste tract beyond which lay truck farms that grew vegetables for much of Brooklyn.

The house was enormous.

It had three whole floors.

Oh, it wasn't really a big house at all, it was quite a small house, but to my eyes, accustomed to an apartment, it was enormous.

And it had those three separate floors, so that even if my mommy and my daddy were home, I might be all alone on a different floor from them.

Or not alone.

That was worse than being alone, a feeling, a kind of dread in my flesh that there was something, or maybe someone, there with me when I was upstairs alone, or alone in the basement.

Worst of all was evening, when shadows piled up on the stairs, and I had to climb up them to bed, pushing through gray mists and veils that concealed—I don't know what, *presences,* always threatening to clutch, to cling, to—I don't know what. Nothing ever reached out and grabbed me; but that didn't dispel the nightly threats, when I lay alone in my bed on that upstairs floor, in the dark, covers pulled up to my chin, to my nose, over my head.

I was afraid of the dark. A light was left burning all night long in the bathroom for me for years. But one weak bulb shining around a corner could not dispel the shadows that threatened me in my shiny new grown-up maple bed.

I really don't want to use the word *ghost,* but it's about the simplest way to describe what I was afraid of. In this freshly plastered and painted box of a brand-new house, I was afraid of ghosts.

That sounds absurd, even to me.

So how would it have sounded to my mother? She was not one to talk to about ghosts. My father? He was hardly ever there when I went to bed. So ghosts, which we all know don't exist, had their way with me at bedtime for years and years and years.

I think, on the whole, I was happiest out of doors, certainly I was on those long, lazy, end-of-summer days, when I lived outside and in perpetual motion, on my tricycle or roller skates or just plain feet, running, jumping, scuffing, hopping, skipping along the sidewalk and around the corner and down the alley.

Restless motion excited and thrilled me. Perhaps it also distracted me from a new and unpleasant perception, which grew within me when I stopped and became still, indoors, a perception of increasing loneliness.

There we were, just two of us, just my mother and me, in that enormous house, almost all the time alone in the house, my mother and me.

And my mother, always distant, always aloof, was now preoccupied in a new way, and shifting somehow, changing in her moods, even in the planes of her face, the contours of her body. Shifting. Changing. More than ever, she was apart from me, and I from her.

Today radios and television sets and record players furnish such houses as mine with the illusion of life, of companionship.

Then there was only the thing itself, undisguised.

Loneliness.

To my not-yet-four-year-old self, it was unaccountable, a sudden spell that blighted my small universe which, before, had been peopled by many figures besides my mother and father, by aunts, uncles, cousins, playmates. Lots and lots of people. And then there were none.

Just my mother.

Of course, the same was true for her, too. She had had other people around, and now she was stuck with me.

And the light of my life, what about him?

Instead of traveling from Flatbush to Manhattan, my father now had to take the subway all the way from Avenue U, practically the country it was then, and it took him more than half an hour longer each way to get to and from his office. And he was seeking additional clients, working longer hours, trying to keep up with the expenses of a new house, because this was 1938, after all, still a deep Depression year, and times were hard. As a general rule, he left the house before I woke up, and arrived home after I'd been put to bed. Days might pass without my seeing my father.

An adult can rationalize such necessity, but what does a child know? Or feel?

Abandonment, that's what. He has forsaken me.

As an infant and toddler, then, I had been used to society. Now, in a brand-new neighborhood, no relatives or friends close by, too young for school, I was plunged into solitude. Perhaps that's where the ghosts came from, some redress, some attempt to people an abruptly empty world. If so, it backfired on me badly.

Ghosts, having appeared, come to stay. And grow to monstrous proportions.

My fourth birthday came and was marked by a wonderful party, at which I wore a striped silk dress with a velvet bodice for which I had had the solitary tantrum of my life, or so, in later years, swore my mother. It was held in the basement. Our house was filled with people. My grandmother came, and assorted cousins, and I remember cake and soda and balloons and my father kissed me good-night on the lips. I was the birthday girl. It was my day. I was four years old.

And the world was bright, and perhaps for a while, the brightness held the ghosts at bay, and the cold and the darkness of winter, and I felt safer.

And then around the turning of the year, an unexpected event came to pass. We were no longer the two of us, my mother and me.

Now we were three.

My baby sister Mindy was born.

You might think that I'd have been delighted: no more ghosts! But it didn't work out that way. The ghosts remained, and the loneliness was worse than before.

There they were, in the big front bedroom, the three of them together, my father, my mother, and *her,* and the door closed firmly against me. My own room, a room for a *big girl,* was a punishment cell, was exile.

Don't be a baby.

Be a *big girl!*

But I wasn't a big girl. I was the same as I had been before she was born.

I had to share with her *my* mommy, *my* daddy, my house, my room, my everything. But even so I took my revenge, and this was it.

I don't remember her *at all.*

I blotted her out of my memory. I paid a price for that, of course. For one thing, during almost the whole of a limbo year, I have no memory of myself, either. I lost myself. Time stood still. At last, after a very long waiting, it began to move again, and I enrolled in kindergarten, and I moved, all by myself, off the world of the block and out into a wider world, one which I didn't have to share with anybody. I went to school. I learned to read. I began to live in the world of books—that is, the world of my imagination.

It was safer there. Books did not betray you, or forget you. Books were always there for you, right where you had left them.

And books gave me a vision, of a land of milk and honey, a land of freedom, a Promised Kingdom. Fairy tales, legends, fantasies; they promised such a vision, and I believed the books. There even existed a place and a time when the promise quickened.

Six days were for laboring, for the reality of the everyday.

On the seventh day there was God, and we exchanged visits.

It's a pretty big thing for God to visit your house.

Oh, during the week I was aware that God existed, at least if I woke up early enough, because then I could watch my father take long thin black leather straps, like ribbon, and coil them around his arm, beginning at the middle finger on his left hand, all the way up and around to his forehead, where the ribbons attached to a little black box, through which he talked to God as he faced a wall and swayed, back and forth, back and forth, droning messages. And he did this every day. Every day. That was one thing devout Jewish men did during the week before going off to work: they talked to God, a faraway God.

That was different from what happened on Friday nights.

On Friday night God himself, actually present, came to visit our house.

My mother spent most of Friday preparing for his visit. She shopped in one store after another, for chickens and fish and challah; and then she stewed and boiled and roasted and baked; and ironed a clean tablecloth, and polished the silver candlesticks and the wine cup and the bread knife, and she set the table for a feast, with a special white satin cover embroidered in colored silk threads to cover the two twisted glossy golden-brown loaves of challah. And everything, *everything,* had to be ready before the first star shone in the evening sky, because after that she lit the candles in the silver candlesticks and then we were in the Sabbath time, the holy time when all work was forbidden. My father and my mother were king and queen, receiving the visit of God, King of all kings, and of his bride, *Shabbat Malkah,* the Sabbath Queen. But somehow the bride was shadowy for me, and easily forgettable, even though her presence was tangible in the silver and crystal and candlelight and food; but God's presence, although totally invisible, was palpable.

So palpable, in fact, as to be oppressive. A mixed blessing, you might say.

There was the grandeur and the awe, on one hand, the chanting of the kiddush, the sweet purple wine and the soft white challah, the delicious food, the singing of grace. But, on the other hand, as the meal came to an end, the shadows gathered thickly in the corners of the room, and the flames of the two Sabbath candles began to flicker, then gutter and go out. Then the familiar terror of the dark with which I lived daily would find me defenseless, because neither I nor anyone else was permitted to turn on the electric lights. God had commanded us not to work on the Sabbath Day, and flicking a light switch on or off was part of the work that was forbidden.

And here he was, right on the spot. Imagine! What would happen if we violated God's commandment right under his very nose?

Unthinkable.

So there I was, frightened and, yes, lonely. Left out. The strength and comfort I might have had from experiencing a God actually present to me in my smallness and fear was lacking, because it was pretty clear to me that God was a grown-up. Or, at any rate, God was *for* grown-ups.

He came to visit in our house, it's true, but primarily to converse with my father who, after all, spoke his language, and seemed on almost equal terms with him. And maybe he spoke to my mother sometimes, although she was so busy serving and washing dishes that I don't know when there would have been time.

But no one, not even me, expected him to have a conversation with me or, later, with my sister. God was a grown-up, and that's who he came to visit and spend his time with. In my bedroom, dark and lonely, God was absent, and I was at the mercy of whatever flourished in God's absence.

Saturdays were better. God, of course, had come to stay with us for

the entire day, which began the previous nightfall, and lasted until
three stars appeared in the Sabbath sky, the signal for the departure of
the Sabbath Queen (whose presence I always forgot about until the
moment of her leaving) and of God.

Saturdays were better primarily, I think, because they were mostly
daylight. On Saturday the God of my father was pretty good, in fact.
You sang songs to him, happy songs with simple choruses even a child
could join in on, and you ate more good food, only it was cold,
because you couldn't turn on the stove either, since turning on the
stove was work. But we could have tea, because my mother always left
one burner on low under an asbestos mat all during the Sabbath, and
the teakettle sat on it and stayed warm.

And very often my father would tell stories at the Sabbath midday
dinner table, stories about his growing up and his adventures.

Oh, we loved those stories. We begged my father to tell them again
and again, with ever-accumulating detail, and gestures, and sound effects.

There were even some terrible stories.

There was the story about the scar under my father's chin, which
he got from a snowball wrapped around a shard of glass, the snowball
thrown at him by the Irish kids two blocks over on the Lower East
Side, who hated Jewish kids and called them Christ-killers. As he told
the story, we would stare under his chin, and trace the scar for ourselves with our forefingers.

We loved my father's stories.

When the last story was told, the cups of tea were finished, the pile
of peanut shells abandoned, my father would go and take a nap, usually
on the sofa, and my mother would finish the dishes, and she would
vanish somewhere. And there I'd be, and my sister. Nothing to do.
No work to do, because work was not allowed on the Sabbath. Work
included playing card games, listening to the radio, turning on a light
to see a book more clearly on a dim wintry afternoon, riding in a car.
What you *could* do was read, until that got boring. Or go for a walk, if
it were nice out. Or you could mope around, and wait for the inter-

minable afternoon to end, and for God to go home so there could be ordinary time again and weekday things, like noise, and light, and activity.

I suppose what I felt is what children of most faiths often feel at especially holy times: God is very holy and very good, but he's not much fun.

And he's remote from little ones.

Yet there is one place I remember as a kind of Eden, although I know with my head that it cannot have been wholly so, one place where God was, and where he revealed himself to me.

On Saturday mornings, when I was five or six, my father would take me by the hand and we would walk the five blocks to the synagogue, not a fancy temple, but a simple *shul,* a plain brick building, like a cube, with a front entrance for the men, and two side entrances for the women, who were relegated to a few rows of benches on either side of the big central block of the one-room shul.

The front door, and the central rows of benches facing the eastern wall, where the ark was, were for men only.

And for me.

Holding my father's hand, I walked with him all the way until we sat together on a wooden bench up front.

Way up front, where God was. That was *his* house, that plain wooden ark, looking like a clothes cabinet, hiding him behind its plain wooden doors, themselves covered by a silken embroidered cloth.

I liked visiting God in his house better than I liked him coming to mine. It was more interesting. And it was somehow different for me in God's house. I didn't feel any separation or remoteness. Awe and mystery, yes, but not separation. I belonged in God's house.

There I was, surrounded by young men, old men with yellowing white beards, middle-aged men, all wearing *yarmulkes*—skullcaps—all wrapped like my father in a *tallith,* a prayer shawl, black stripes on creamy fabric, long fringes dripping from the shawls, fringes with which my father would tickle my palm. My father would point with his forefinger at the Hebrew letters in the *siddur,* the prayer book, so that I too could follow the service.

And then everyone would rise—the men in their prayer shawls, their young sons, the few women at the edges of the room, and me, lifted up in my father's arms—and the rabbi would open the doors of the ark, and there it was, shining out, resplendent, the light which was the presence of God, his *Shekinah,* his glory, which dwelt in the ark, and from which I knew to avert my eyes, lest I be stricken by the brightness, a radiance so holy it was unsafe to do more than peek at it.

And then would be lifted out from the ark one of the great Torahs, dressed in velvet and satin and adorned with silver breastplates and *rimmonim*—ornamental silver pomegranates that topped the two wooden handles of each scroll—trimmed with tiny silver bells, so that it jingled sweetly as it was tenderly lifted out, and that was God's voice, as the dazzling silver light was his radiance.

Then the Torah was paraded around the room, to be touched and kissed by outstretched fingers, male and female, jostling to come close to the aisle where the procession passed, or else holy books, *siddurim,* were touched to it, and the edges of prayer shawls, and then the books and the shawls were kissed, so that profane fingers should not outrage the precious body of the scroll. But I always touched the velvet itself with my fingers, whenever I could.

Then the Torah would be tenderly undressed, and lifted up, and reverenced in a rising swell of chanted Hebrew, and then it was un-rolled, and read aloud by the rabbi, or by a reader, while someone held a tiny silver hand with a pointed finger to mark the reader's place among uninflected Hebrew characters inscribed sharp and black and mysterious on rich cream parchment.

And when the reading was finished, the scroll would be dressed again, and lifted on high, and everyone would rise as, in a perfect storm of chanting and singing, the Torah was returned to the ark, and the doors were closed and the radiance shut away again, and God was once more safely hidden.

Invisible, but present. Always present.

On Simchat Torah, a holiday especially beloved of children, all the Torahs were taken out from the ark, and, glittering silver bells jingling, around and around the one-room shul they were carried, and after them streamed all the little children, and the middle-sized children, boys and girls still undifferentiated at that age, all waving blue-and-white paper flags bearing the star of David, long before anyone stamping down the aisles ever dreamed that there would actually someday be a state of Israel. And on the top of the stick of each paper flag would be impaled an apple, for sweetness.

Taste and see the goodness of the Lord.

Simchat Torah, the joyful celebration, the rejoicing for the gift of the Torah, God's book.

His holy words.

In the beginning was the Word.

That's the first word of the Hebrew Scriptures, *bereshit,* in the beginning.

John's gospel begins: In the beginning was the Word.

First of all, God spoke. He spoke the universe into being. The Torah *was,* before the world was created.

As Jesus *was,* before the world was created, Jesus the Word, who dwells in an ark, in a tabernacle, covered sometimes by an embroidered cloth. And when the tabernacle is opened, and the hosts (which are the wafers changed into the body of Christ, who is the Word) are taken out and displayed, all rise, or kneel, because God is present.

A burning light always marks the presence of God, at home in his tabernacle.

In the synagogue, the Eternal Flame burns in a red holder, while in a Catholic church the vigil light that marks the presence of the consecrated host can gleam red, or yellow, or white.

When I would go to church, morning after morning, for the nine long months of becoming a Catholic, to watch the celebration of the Eucharist in which I could not participate, I noticed—because I noticed everything in those days, the air seemed thinner, and everything stood out sharply—that people, when they entered the church, would genuflect before they sat down on the wooden benches that I learned to call pews.

I thought they were genuflecting to the huge crucifix at the front of the church, a kind of paying their respects to Christ there. But one day, as I sat and looked up at the crucifix (which was for a long, long time a scandal to my eyes), my attention was somehow caught by the gold-colored box below it, resting on a marble table.

And suddenly I knew.

That was what they were genuflecting to, not the crucifix. *That* was the ark in which the Shekinah was hidden, the radiance, the body which is the Word. No one told me that. I just knew it.

The Shekinah was there.

It called to me. And I recognized it by the movement of my heart.

The stereopticon experience, two images converging to become a single multidimensional picture, happened to me again and again in my slow and painful journey. But it was perhaps most vivid in that moment when the eyes of my heart recognized that beyond boundaries, beyond appearances, beyond categories, these two bodies were somehow One Body.

The proudest affirmation of the Jewish faith, the first Jewish words I learned, were the *Shema,* the central creed of Judaism.

Shema Yisroel, Adonai Elohenu, Adonai Echod.

Hear, O Israel, the Lord our God, the Lord is One.

And I did believe, passionately, in the one God of the holy time, the sacramental God of my father.

Only—

That God was too far away.

With the close of the Sabbath, God departed for the remote high heavens, taking his Sabbath Queen with him, and then the week began; and that weekly world, my everyday world, the one in which I lived and moved and had my being, was ruled by other gods, earthy gods, underground gods, the gods of my mother, household idols which she, like Rachel in the Scriptures, had brought with her, secretly, from her father's house. And they were gods, not of light, however blinding, but gods of darkness.

Household Idols

*T*HE TRUTH IS THAT MY father's God played a limited role in my world, time-limited and space-limited. When he retired to the synagogue or somewhere up in the highest heavens, my world was dominated by vastly different powers.

My mother's gods.

The God of my father had a Hebrew name, *Adonai,* so sacred that, unless one were praying, one had to call him *Adoshem,* lest one profane the holy name. And in English, he was "God."

But my mother's gods were so darkly powerful that they were never even called by name at all. The gods that really mattered, day in, day out, were faceless, nameless, implacable powers for whom my mother was a priestess. Oh, I *believed* in my father's God; but he was of no help or comfort or protection to me in the absence of my father. Day in, day out, it was the household idols of my mother whom I learned to fear and to worship and to obey.

What were they like?

Dangerous, of course. I can feel the old wariness inhibiting my pen right now. It's dangerous even to *speak* of them, to draw their attention in any way at all.

What I am telling you about is my early *Weltanschauung*. That's a fancy German word for "world view."

No matter what we call it, even if we are unaware of having one, we all do have a world view. It's our philosophy, our answer to a universal existential human question, What's the world about? What kind of world is it? And our personal philosophy, flowing from that original Weltanschauung, answers the personal existential question, What is *my life* about?

It is the nature of our gods which determines our Weltanschauung, our world view.

What kind of gods do we worship?

That is a vital question.

What kind of gods did I worship, week in, week out?

My world view was adopted so long ago and renounced so recently that, if you were to ask me, Do you still believe in it? I would have to answer, No, but sometimes I forget.

The God I choose to worship now is a God of Love.

But then I bowed down to gods of dread, of doom, of malice, of caprice.

How can I explain?

They weren't demons or monsters or alien creatures, nothing so cozy as that, or so tangible. Isaac Bashevis Singer writes about such demons, who romped about and plagued the vanished shtetls of Eastern Europe. My mother's household idols, the ones she brought with her from the house of her father, came from those same shtetls.

But they were invisible, impersonal, implacable, and omnipresent, true gods (of a type), begotten, not made, one in being with my mother, through whom all things, especially me, were made. Through her came salvation, or such safety as was possible, to be sought after daily.

Doom threatened daily, had to be averted daily.

My world, then, reflecting the nature of these gods, was a world of dread and constant threat, malicious intentionality, capricious disaster, a dangerous world, a world in which Something Terrible was surely going to happen because Something Terrible is *always* going to happen.

Watch out or your face will freeze that way.

Am I compulsive still?

If you sing before breakfast, you'll cry before supper.

Driven?

Pick up the penny, put it in your shoe and wear it all day for good luck, because if you don't—

Suspicious?

Don't talk about the movie you're looking forward to, or the birthday party, or the good grade—

See, you were in a hurry and you fell, God punished you.

My paternal grandmother hears my baby sister's beauty praised, and she spits, pooh pooh pooh.

Even my grandmother knows my mother's gods: *they* are jealous of human beauty.

Don't plan anything. *They* are jealous of human happiness.

Don't praise anything. *They* are jealous of human accomplishment.

Don't boast, or rejoice, don't speak of any good thing, or *they* will hear you.

These are jealous gods, easily bored, ready to meddle and interfere.

Old World Italians and Jews share one concept, which they call, in their respective mother tongues, *malocchio,* or *keinahurrah.*

Ken ayin hara. Without an evil eye.

You should be without an evil eye.

So Italian grandmothers make the sign of the horns, index finger and little finger pointed, to ward off the evil eye. And Jewish grandmothers spit, pooh pooh pooh—to blind it?—and hang red ribbons on the baby carriage to deter the demons.

But our powers had no name. They could be warded off by certain ritual gestures—the penny in the shoe, the pulled left ear, the bitten tongue—but there was no universal remedy against evil. Only a whole complicated arsenal, each remedy specific against only one particular disaster, a complicated pharmacopoeia for a small girl to master.

A magical world.

Maybe you laugh at all of this. Scorn it as superstition, ridiculous nonsense. Maybe it is. But imagine *believing* it, as my mother did.

I *believed* that if I ill-wished anyone with my words or even in my thoughts, and I didn't bite my tongue right away, something terrible would happen to them.

To this day, if I ill-wish someone in my most fleeting thought, my tongue darts between my teeth in a reflexive action, bypassing brain and volition, compulsively repeating, I believe.

So, do I still believe?

No.

But sometimes I forget. And my body remembers.

Pull your left ear!

Bite your tongue!

My father liked to call my mother a gypsy, for her dark hair and dark eyes and love of dancing.

I knew she was a gypsy because she could divine the future.

She could read palms, and tea-leaves, and tell fortunes with cards.

Not a game, but really read the future in them.

You spilled the salt, pick it up with your right hand and throw it over your left shoulder or you'll have a fight.

I *believed* it.

Your nose itches? You're going to have a fight with somebody.

Prophecies of doom.

The world, for my mother, was a dark place of powers out of control, of malevolent intent. My thoroughly modern mother, born in America. This, then, was her inheritance: the fear, and the ways to combat it. And she strove, as best she could, to protect me from those dangerous powers by teaching me her skills, her lures, her arts, as quickly as she could.

And I was a quick learner.

But this inheritance of a world in which Something Terrible is always going to happen was a double inheritance for me.

It was not only the wisdom of my mother.

It was the magisterium of my father.

Dread was our "family myth," to use a fashionable sociological phrase.

My superstitious mother believed in picking up pins and pulling ears and biting tongues.

My superrational lawyer father shared my mother's view of a world of dread. Their shared vision was a European shtetl vision of pogroms and calamities and exiles, a black and bleak universe where every man's hand is raised against the Jew, as it was in the beginning, is now, and ever shall be, world without end, a curse rather than a blessing.

But he could take no comfort in gestures or signs, because he scorned such things as nonsense.

The only remedy, then, for a rational person at the mercy of a dark universe, lies in perfection. Which means being perfectly logical, thinking everything through, foreseeing all, forestalling all. He built elaborate constructions of thought in which to cage amorphous evil, to shine a white light upon it, and by predicting it, drain its power.

The lawyerly way.

His Weltanschauung was as ominous and despairing as my mother's was, but it was more plausible, it conformed better to the rational world.

Magic is for nut cases; reason is respectable.

They were both so afraid, they only wanted to protect us. How could they know?

Once a year they came together, their two Weltanschauungs of pessimism and dread, once a year the superstitious, fatalistic mother and the ultra-rational, skeptical father united in expressing their anxieties and fears.

It was on Yom Kippur, when the shofar was blown to reach God's ears, and alert him to good Jews' intentions for the coming year, and their repentance for the bad actions of the past one.

On Yom Kippur the warding-off is spelled out.

Repentance, prayer, and righteousness can avert the evil decree.

And, in a unanimity that breached the abyss between emotion and reason, my parents were for once united in their translation of that remedy.

Pessimism, worry, and *ritual observance* can avert the evil decree.

Dwelling on evil consequences suffices as repentance. Constant worry is prayer enough. Thinking hard enough, pulling left ears, biting tongues, these are acts of righteousness.

Avinu Malkenu.

Our Father, Our King.

I have sinned before you.

Yom Kippur, Day of Awe, Day of Atonement.

Pessimism.

Pardon us, forgive us, take away our sin.

Worry.

The final shofar blast, long and sharp and piercing.

Ritual observance.

My father's God, my mother's gods, united for once in a single vision as we emerge, cleansed and shriven, into the starry evening.

Tonight nothing terrible will happen.

Tonight all the gods are satisfied.

All is well tonight.

Until tomorrow.

The Wages of Sin

AMONG THE SPECIFIC "TERRIBLE THINGS" that were going to happen, and, in fact, often did happen, was sickness. This was back in the days when doctors made house calls because their presence was the best, and often the only, medicine they had to offer, the days before tetracycline or penicillin or even sulfa drugs, when polio scourged the nation every summer and strep throats were killers.

The dark and ominous gods of my mother were quite equal to the task of bringing about sickness, as well as other disasters. Indeed, this is an ancient function ascribed to gods. Even to the God of my father, who, in the Book of Exodus, is reported to have sent among the whining, complaining, backward-yearning Israelites in the desert a plague of stinging serpents so effective that very soon he had to prompt Moses to build a brazen serpent mounted on a staff to display to the plague-stricken as an antidote, or the Scriptures might very well have ended right then in that very book, chapter and verse.

Malignant diseases, such as cancer, derive that adjective from a personalized perception: just as *malevolent* means, literally, ill, or evil-wishing, *malignant* means to have an evil disposition toward others. Cancer holds a personal animus toward its victim, according to this etymology, which is also the view held by many, perhaps most cancer victims. It seems to be a universal tendency among humans to seek out the etiology of disease and sickness, and to find its cause most frequently in a personalized context.

If you have a nonscientific mind, which I do, you begin with the *effect* of an illness, and then start casting about for a plausible and convincing cause. Even though the gods were involved in much sickness, the responsibility for them was shared by human beings. The responsibility for averting the evil decree is in good part ours, and illness represents punishment for failures not so much of sanitation or of hygiene, but *moral* failures, like carelessness, disobedience, willfulness, foolishness.

How do you get a cold? You catch it.

Volition.

Cousin Buddy should never have corn, said the doctor, but his mother gave him corn and he had a fit and he got retarded from it, so the *immediate* cause was the corn, but the *real* cause was Aunt Dora's carelessness and disobedience, and God punished her because Buddy got retarded. Simple logic.

Some more examples.

I wore glasses because I had made my eyes weak by reading when I had the measles even though my mother told me not to. One can also ruin one's eyes by reading in bad light. *Everybody* knows that.

I got acne from eating the wrong foods, and too much candy; and I'm short because I didn't eat enough when I was little.

Look, for all we know, maybe those reasons are *true.* Germs may, or may not, be accepted as an explanation of illness. But they are never a *sufficient* explanation for us.

The point is that most of our everyday garden-variety illnesses, by this theory, are caused by something *we* have done. Or not done. And therefore what we need is forgiveness.

Why else does Jesus say to the paralyzed man, Your sins are forgiven, get up and walk?

I found sickness and disease fascinating, in the dual sense of *attractive*
and *frightening*. And so I began young to learn about disease, because I
was fascinated with it, and because learning about it gave me the
illusion of having some sort of control over it. Education and intellectual activity are very good for that, for giving the illusion of control.

My favorite reading was—

Perhaps it's more accurate to say, my *obsessive* reading, was a thick
pamphlet put out by the United States Department of Labor, in its role
as forerunner of the Department of Health, Education and Welfare.
(And between those two names lies an entire history and philosophy,
doesn't it?) Anyway, the pamphlet discussed the most common and
serious childhood diseases, their causes to whatever extent that was
known, their incubation period, symptoms, duration, and prognosis.
What fascinated me the most—*mysterium tremendum et fascinans*—were
never the ordinary things, mumps, or chicken pox, but the really serious ones, the diseases whose morbidity (like my own) was high. I
knew everything the Department of Labor knew about polio, menin-
gitis, smallpox, and leprosy. Every time I was sick, I checked out my
symptoms against the killers. And I always found a dangerous symp-
tom—

When I was seven or eight years old, there were precious few reme-
dies for these illnesses. Description of disease was the state of the art,
not cure. My reading was really scary stuff.

Being sick, actively sick, in those days was awful: the pain of sore
throats or earaches unrelieved by antibiotics, the relentless high fevers,
the real fears and anxieties of parents and children alike, because children *did* die then, much more readily than now.

Convalescence, however, was a whole lot better. Now, our kids get
the latest magic pill or potion, return to seeming health within a day,
and back to school they go. But surely their systems aren't *cured* of the
bugs in a day. Only camouflaged.

We, on the other hand, *luxuriated* in convalescence. We got special tasty invalid diets, and could listen to all the radio programs. And we could play with paper dolls and read.

My obsession with the mysterious nature of illness has been life-long. My favorite reading, once I outgrew the United States Department of Labor pamphlet, was real-life mystery stories like the discovery of insulin by Banting, or Dr. Ehrlich's magic bullet that snuffed out syphilis. I devoured Paul Henry de Kruif's *Microbe Hunters,* and anything resembling it. No novel, no mystery story could touch the suspense and power for me of these narratives of etiology.

I was fascinated by epidemics of all kinds.

When my mother took out *Forever Amber* from the drugstore's lending library (that was the first, and, no doubt, the tamest of the "respectable" dirty books) and then found me curled up in the basement reading it, she screamed and yelled and sent me right away to bring it back to the drugstore. My mother was wrong. I wasn't interested in steamy sex scenes. They were boring, and I doubt if I understood them. What I was engrossed in were the pages and pages of detailed, horrific descriptions of the Black Death, bubonic plague.

Much later still that same interest in disease led me to psychology, to Theodor Reik, to Karen Horney, to Freud.

And to dreams, and to Jung, and much, much later, to my own psychotherapy; which, in order even to enter upon, I had for many years to confront mocking, scornful figures from my own past.

Go to a crazy doctor?

Such was the view of diseases of the mind and psychiatry in my household.

So I'm crazy, I guess.

You think all this theory of causality I've been describing is crazy, too? That it comes from the Dark Ages? You think we're more humane now? That we don't blame victims?

Look around you, friend.

"Natural" causes aren't enough for us, either. Or why else do we have to come up with "Type A" behavior as a cause of heart attacks? And repressed stress, bottling up our feelings, as a cause of cancer? You don't think that's not a guilt trip? *Of course* we teach that sickness is caused by behavior, just like the bad old days. You smoked, so you got emphysema, I told you so. You screwed someone of the same sex, you got AIDS, I told you so. Lyme disease? I told you not to walk in the woods.

That's not "natural" causes, that's behavior, that's guilt trips. You know what that is? That's SIN.

You did it. By your carelessness, disobedience, willfulness, foolishness.

Back where we began.

AIDS and herpes are manna from heaven for the moralists, and the wages of sin are still death.

Now *that's* crazy.

But when I was making hospital chaplaincy visits, I found that again and again people—the patient usually, but sometimes a relative— would be in anguish: What did I do to deserve this? It must have been because . . .

Those who hadn't banished the old-fashioned vocabulary of sin from their lives often found that confession to a priest, and absolution, could bring about small miracles of healing, if not of the body, then of the spirit, an increase of strength, at least of inner strength.

But that brings us to the subject of miracles, which for most of my life I had given up belief in; and so, certain comforts and solaces will have to wait unacknowledged because, at the time of which I am writing and for a long time to come, and for too many people I know who still believe in these things: the Wages of Sin are Death.

And *nothing* could avert that evil decree.

Worlds at War

*J*UST BEFORE 8 A.M. on Sunday, December 7, 1941, Japanese bombers roared down on Pearl Harbor. Brooklyn clocks read almost 2:30 in the afternoon, at which time my family was visiting at a cousin's apartment.

I don't remember at what time the unsuspecting adults, turning on the radio to hear the increasingly gloomy news from Europe, were stunned by the news of the Japanese surprise attack. What I *do* remember is that we children were hustled into our winter coats and hats and leggings earlier than usual, because it was important to get back home before—before the world ended, I suppose.

My real memory of that day, the day that Franklin Roosevelt promised would live in infamy, is of the back seat of the car, driving home through chilly dusky Brooklyn streets, huddled face down on the floor frozen in terror, listening for the sound of planes overhead, waiting for the bombs to drop and explode on the nape of my neck.

I was seven years old, and scared to death.

Of course, seven-year-olds don't stay permanently scared to death.

When, after a week or two, no bombs fell, and the routine of life continued essentially unchanged, I breathed more deeply, and relaxed into my everyday existence as a second-grader in P.S. 206.

What the war meant at school was air-raid drills in which we huddled under our desks for a while, and then, at the sound of the all-clear siren, emerged and resumed our lessons where we had left off. The war also meant plastic identification disks, which we wore around our necks hung by bits of cord. We quickly grew used to wearing the disks, and seldom speculated on the grim possibilities they represented.

To be patriotic, you saved gum-wrapper linings for tin-foil drives at school, smoothed them out and offered them up in homeroom for the war effort. We were confident that, somehow, our little scraps of tin would heap one upon another until they made a huge enough mass to rain down as bombs upon the Japs, our yellow enemy.

We recited the Pledge of Allegiance daily with increased fervor, and sang "The Star-Spangled Banner" in assembly every Friday (at least the notes within our singing range) with gusto.

My school years at P.S. 206 were ordinary times of lessons and recess and gym and assembly. After school there was homework, and jump-rope and ball-bouncing games and jacks and potsy (which is a Brooklyn variant of hopscotch) and stoop ball and roller-skating and bike riding. Some of these activities were sex-segregated; for instance, jump rope was for girls, and ball-bouncing games and jacks. Only boys could play marbles and stickball.

Every day during baseball season I listened to Red Barber, in his southern drawl, retail the misadventures of the Brooklyn Dodgers, because that's the way it was. If you lived in Brooklyn, you rooted for the Brooklyn Dodgers, and that was that. They were Dem Bums in those days, perpetual losers, and we loved them. Another war that passionately engaged me, as it engaged an entire borough, was the war between the Brooklyn Dodgers and their archrivals, the New York Giants.

When we got older, Saturdays were movie days. For a quarter

(which I had to give to a friend the day before so I would not be guilty of the sin of carrying money or purchasing tickets on the Sabbath) we would see a double feature. There were occasional war movies of heroism and sacrifice; I remember crying over the sufferings of our brave allies in *Song of Russia*. There was always a newsreel, Movietone News, or Paramount, The Eyes and the Ears of the World, and in those Hitler ranted, or Mussolini, and tanks advanced amidst bursting shells. And, inevitably, there was the reassuring presence of Franklin D. Roosevelt, President of the United States, and, for me, God's surrogate on earth.

When the long afternoon matinee was over, we emerged into the familiar surroundings of Avenue U. The war, with its black-and-white soldiers and sailors, its heroes and villains, was left behind us in the movie theater. We returned to our ordinary lives.

You see, that was the way it was. We children were as jingoistic in our talk as anyone could desire. But our patriotism, so fervent, was shallow; and, as astonishing as it may seem now, our neighborhood was an island, and we, my friends and I, led an insular life. Insular, and insulated.

And that was the war as I experienced it, living in the Avenue U section of Brooklyn.

By night the war took on a different reality.

The night brought bad dreams.

And the blackout.

Everyone had to have special blackout curtains; and volunteer wardens patrolled the neighborhood with swaddled flashlights, as soon as dusk fell, knocking at the door of anyone whose skimpy or carelessly drawn blackout curtains permitted even the smallest ray of light to penetrate the darkness, thereby guiding enemy planes straight to our neighborhood. The moon, always an ambivalent symbol, became on the nights of her fullness an unequivocal enemy, a quisling, illuminating our hiding places with her cold white light.

The bombs always threatened, but never came. Daylight always returned, and with it, ordinary life.

So, for me, the world at war was almost indistinguishable from a world at peace.

It is not true, however, that I was unacquainted with warfare.

Far from it.

The warfare I knew intimately was fought on a different scale, waged in a different style, no less terrible for all that, but perhaps more so, because it was waged right inside my own house, by combatants whom I knew well.

My house was a battlefield in a war I quickly came to view as a universal one—the War Between Men and Women. This domestic warfare, with its guerrilla skirmishes and sudden outbreaks, was part of the everyday fabric of my life. Oh, there were truces, it *couldn't* have been constant, not even in my selective memory, and much of the time one combatant, my father, had withdrawn from the battle zone to the neutral territory of his office.

What was this war about?

In every war, large or little, issues are made to seem simple, preferably monolithic.

The Civil War was fought over slavery.

But in reality issues are always complex; and the situation was no different in the ongoing war between my mother and my father. I am no different from any other news commentator, I am reporting only from the outside, even though the warring parties were my own parents, and we all lived together in the same house.

I don't know the *whys,* but I can tell you *what* I witnessed. First, the raised voices, the shouting matches, mercifully muffled for me by my obligingly poor memory.

That was the hot war, waged with angry words.

Such brief and noisy incidents were succeeded by a cold war, infinitely more terrible, whose weapons were icy politeness and communication through channels.

Tell your mother I'm going out for a walk.

Ask your father if he wants anything else to eat.

Not surrogate messages, carried from one room to another; but false ones, deliberately uttered in the same room, seated around the same table.

Bad as that was, the not-speaking was the worst. Long silences chilled the very life of the house, hours of it, sometimes a day or two or more.

Silence is a terrible weapon.

I learned that early; and it increased my natural tendency to chatter, to say something, *anything,* to fill up the silence that dragged like leaden anchors at my spirit.

What did they fight *about?*

Not about alcoholism or gambling, not about other women, or other men.

Nothing so terrible, then. Not really. Just arguments over things that don't matter, questions of style, simple things.

Simple things which, to my mind are the really vital things. The daily exchanges, the simple tasks.

I remember my father's nagging; I remember my mother's sullen unresponsiveness. He *would* that she would—but she *would not.*

The truth is that they were incompatible.

East and West, oil and water.

But I elevated this particular case to a universal principle.

This, I thought, is how men and women relate to one another.

I concluded that the natural condition of men and women was warfare. That men and women were, in the natural condition, enemies.

The images.

My mother, standing through a long Friday night Sabbath meal, holding the basin for my seated father to wash his hands, offering him a towel, serving the fish, the soup, chicken, dessert, darting between dining room and kitchen, then washing the dishes. And a repeat performance on Saturday.

The image of the king and the handmaiden. Traditional images.

I can now agree that such an image is not necessarily antithetical to love.

But my mother would serve just as meekly when she was furious, when she was "not speaking to" my father, her demeanor at total odds with the feelings seething inside her. Come what may, she would fulfil her marital obligation.

Do her duty.

And in bed?

I have no idea.

In public, that is, in front of their children, there was no demonstrativeness. I never remember seeing them hug or kiss, or touch one another in passing in the way that is more intimate even than hugs or kisses. I never saw physical tenderness.

And I never heard either of them say, to each other, or to us, I'm sorry.

I sometimes was made to say, I'm sorry. But it was always *pro forma,* because I was *made* to, not because I felt repentant. I said it to allow normal life to run on again, and it was only words. It was never, ever, a turning of the heart.

And my parents never said it at all. Nor did they display it in gesture, or touch.

Fights ended by attrition, or boredom; and the issues were never addressed.

So I grew up believing that *I'm sorry* is only words, that there is no such thing as repentance. And so, for me, there wasn't. I have learned, the hard way, and only late in life, that real repentance is possible, but only in the presence of forgiveness.

And vice versa.

Without repentance there cannot be forgiveness, and without forgiveness, it is not possible to repent.

Oh, with God all things are possible. We are forgiven in the instant of our repentance.

But our relations with one another are more problematic. They need *I'm sorry,* and *I forgive you.* In my house there was neither forgiving nor being forgiven. Like World War Two, the terms were simple: unconditional surrender.

So the war ground on, never-ending. This war waged, as I saw it, not between one particular man and woman, but between all men and all women.

My father and my mother loved one another. The problem was that they could never agree on what that meant, to love. The freedoms, the responsibilities. The terms of love, and its expression. That was what was at stake in this war.

And there are no fair ways in which this particular war can be waged. They are all foul.

Ancillary to the main issue of the war was a side issue, namely, the allegiance of the children.

Whose partisans would we be, my sister and I?

My parents fought for our hearts in subtle and overt ways.

But we spent far more time with my mother than with my father, so she had a great tactical advantage.

She would take us out for lunch, for instance, and order a bacon, lettuce, and tomato sandwich for us, or to a Chinese restaurant, where we would have chicken chow mein, spareribs, egg roll, all of which were forbidden to us, and which therefore we adored as special treats. We were Orthodox Jews, my mother kept a strictly kosher home, and bacon was *treyf,* as was food prepared in a nonkosher restaurant. So she would take us out for these wonderful special treats, and then, as their price, swear us to secrecy.

Don't tell your father, he'll be mad.

Were we aware of her subtle attack on him through us?

We were too greedy. And too young. Just as she was too unconscious to recognize her own motives, the handmaiden taking her revenge on the king she served. And so these repeated silent lies made us her coconspirators, bound us to her in pleasure and in guilt, corrupted our relation with our father, alienated us from him.

Why did she marry him?

The truth is probably that, in my mother's day and circumstance, women got married, and that was that.

Having married, they stayed married.

Divorce was unthinkable.

And so the silence at the heart of our house, at the heart of my parents' marriage, was not a void, but a container of the unspoken, unthinkable, unsayable words that resonated in the silence.

You are not what I expected. . . .

You are not what I wanted. . . .

You disappoint me. . . .

I want a divorce. . . .

Unthinkable!

And so our family stood—ask anyone!—foursquare, then, after my youngest sister's birth, fivesquare, solid, eternal, like a cast sculpture, strong and ringing to the touch, but at its heart, hollow.

How did we civilians survive in that charged and menacing and deafening silence?

I don't know about my sister. Perhaps it was her dolls that she clung to. Me, I took refuge in school, in friends, in books, in the basement or in the bathroom with my books.

Some years later, after one really horrible fight between them, a reversion to the hottest of shooting wars followed by a cold war that had seemed to go on forever, my father took me aside on his lap to reassure me. (I must have been twelve or thirteen; and that was very unusual for him, he had stopped holding me on his lap years before.)

I didn't have to worry, he said. They wouldn't be divorcing, no matter how bad this fight was. If we didn't divorce right in that first year, he said, when we fought all the time, we won't divorce now.

He explained that they had refrained from a divorce then because they had me on the way, and then there I was, a helpless baby, he told me, so of course they had to stay together for my sake.

I was devastated.

I never told him so. I never even allowed myself to think too closely about it. But with those words of his, I took upon myself the whole burden of my parents' lives, of their marriage, of their unhappiness together. Upon my back I took it, and so I became another casualty in the never-ending war being waged on my own home front, the War, as I saw it, Between Men and Women.

Changes

*I*T WAS ON APRIL 12, 1945, that my cyclic world of childhood, a child's world of frozen time, was abruptly shattered.

God erupted into my ancestors' history when he called out Abraham from his cyclic world into linear time. For me history intervened and linear time began on that Thursday when, for me and for many thousands of children like me, God died.

On April 12, in Warm Springs, Georgia, in the presence of the mistress the public knew nothing about, President Franklin Delano Roosevelt was stricken with a massive cerebral hemorrhage, and died.

Franklin Delano Roosevelt had been the only President of the United States my friends and I had ever known, he was our parents' hero and the savior and bulwark of the Western world against the forces of the devil himself in the form of Hitler and his allies. And now he was dead.

The sixteenth- and seventeenth-century concept of the divine right of kings seems absurd to our rational, democratic twentieth-century society.

Childish.

Well, perhaps so. But it is understandable to me because that is exactly what I believed in my child's heart, without ever putting it into words: Franklin Delano Roosevelt was God's emissary on earth.

For me, his death meant that a piece of God had died. A basic security was broken, the world would never be the same again.

Nor was it.

Scarcely a month later, early in May, came V-E Day, and the end of the European War. And another death: first God's emissary died, and now so did the Great Satan Himself, Hitler.

Great events heaped upon great events! Before the summer of 1945 was over, two atomic bombs had been dropped on Japan, the first mushroom clouds to loom on our horizon, but in those far-off, naive times, they were simply and purely symbols of triumph and victory. Days later, Japan surrendered, and Brooklyn erupted in a frenzy of celebration.

V-J Day!

There were block parties everywhere, platters of delicatessen and galvanized wash buckets filled with ice and soda, cakes made from hoarded sugar, trestle tables set out; all up and down Avenue U people danced in the street, friends and neighbors and even strangers hugged and kissed and danced in the street, men in uniform were mobbed and adored, the world went wild with joy.

The war was over!

We had no churches in our neighborhood, so we didn't hear any church bells ring out. But there were car horns honking, and fire engine sirens, and noisemakers, and streamers, and shouting and stamping of feet, a gigantic Purim festival, or so it seemed to me, when everyone, not just Jews, drowned out the name of Haman (for which read Hitler) and celebrated God's triumph over the enemies of his chosen people, a time of pure celebration, rejoicing unalloyed.

Now the prophecy had come true, they had beat the swords into ploughshares, and every man could sit under his vine and his fig tree, and none shall make him afraid, nor shall they study war any more.

No more war.

From now on, time was linear, and while it could dawdle, it could no longer stand still, or merely go round and round. September came, and Labor Day, and back-to-school.

All these great events in the Great World outside Brooklyn presaged major upheavals in my personal life during 1946. I began a new school, Cunningham Junior High School, that fall; a baby sister named Jessica was born that winter; but from the point of view of *this* story, the most significant shift occurred, along a predictable fault line, in the synagogue in the fall of 1946.

For the previous two years, I had gone in the afternoon twice a week to Hebrew school to learn the prayer book. I loved the Hebrew letters, their exotic shapes, their sonorous sounds, the little crowns and tails that adorned them. I was a quick study, a natural student, and so I was usually the best in the class, better than any of the boys.

All the other Hebrew students in my class were boys.

I didn't think much about why that might be. It was enough that my father wanted me to be able to read and write Hebrew.

When this new year began for us twelve-year-olds, however, my parents were asked to remove me from the Hebrew class. There was no more point, they—whoever "they" specifically were—explained. From now on lessons were preparation for bar mitzvah, the ritual entry of a thirteen-year-old into the adult Jewish community.

A thirteen-year-old *boy's* entry.

Only a boy's entry.

Since I was a girl, I could not be bar mitzvah, and since I would not be bar mitzvah, I didn't belong in the class any more, so I had to go. Q.E.D.

So that is how I was dropped out of Hebrew school.

Simultaneously it was made clear to my father and to me that I was no longer welcome to sit in the men's section of the sanctuary, up front, before the ark. From now on, if I chose to go to shul with my father on Saturday mornings, I would have to leave him at the front door, enter by the side door, and sit by myself in the women's section.

My mother didn't go to services on ordinary Saturdays. Very few women did, and most of them were elderly, strangers to me, among whom I felt as out of place as the men felt I was now among them.

And what could women do, anyway?

More to the point, what could women *not* do?

They could not wrap themselves in prayer shawls, they could not sit near the ark, they could not come forward to read the blessings before the reading of the Torah and Haftorah portions.

They could not even be counted.

If there were twenty women present in the shul for services, and only nine men, there couldn't be a service, because in order to have a service there must be a *minyan,* and a *minyan* is ten men.

Men.

Women cannot be counted.

Women don't count.

How did I feel about this banishment?

I accepted, because that's the way it was, growing up female and Jewish in America in the forties—

Jews like to make it sound good, you know.

They talk in terms of loving concern: women mustn't be burdened with responsibilities and demands of ritual and prayer lest those interfere with women's primary duties, child-rearing and homemaking, the most sacred, the most honored, of all duties.

If Orthodox Jews truly hold women and womanly obligations in the high esteem they claim, how come the prescribed daily prayer of every Orthodox Jewish man includes one of gratitude for not having been born a woman?

And what if a woman *prefers* the ritual, the prayers, the minutiae of observance? *Wants* to assume the obligations? Wants to count? To be counted?

Mind you, we are not talking about *options:* you can do it later, after the household is fed; or, you can do it later when you're older.

No. We are talking about the *permanent* exclusion of women from full participation in the holy mysteries of public worship.

The way I look at it is that men get the goodies, and women get stuck with the shit details.

Sure, somebody's got to do it.

But then don't dress up a necessity in the guise of care and kindness and privilege. Don't *spiritualize* the necessity.

Don't tell me it was God in his goodness who ordained it, because I don't believe that. I don't believe in such a male chauvinist God.

Not that I hold any brief for other religions, sects, and denominations. They almost all subordinate and denigrate women as cruelly as Judaism. But my first anger is for Judaism, because I was a Jewish girl, and this is what I lived.

Why didn't my father protest? Why did he assent in my betrayal? He too saw it as women's inevitability, I suppose. At any rate, my place was now in the women's section of the shul, and I went only at the high holidays. Most of the time I didn't even go inside, but with the other prepubescent girls hung around the unpaved area outside, wearing brand-new dresses, gossiping and giggling and waiting for *the boys* to join us—the boys showing off, making scornful comments about our looks or our dresses or pointedly turning their backs on us, and we in turn would toss insults at them or tease them.

When the teasing and the flirting lost their savor, the boys returned to the sanctuary, to the ark, to the davening, and continued their initiation into the male mysteries they were about to inherit. We girls went on hanging around outside, bored, cross, out of sorts, waiting for our mothers to emerge and go home and prepare the midday meal so that it would be ready to serve to the husbands, fathers, Lords of the Sabbath, upon their arrival.

At that long-ago time when I was only almost twelve, I simply accepted as women's inevitability the decree forbidding my participation in full synagogue worship. I turned my thoughts to other things, and sank my anger deep into unconsciousness, whence it surfaced in 1979, when my husband and I were touring in Jerusalem. One Saturday, toward dusk, walking through the old Jewish quarter, our small tour group and guide entered one of the few synagogues remaining after intensive shelling in the 1967 war. This particular synagogue is called the "Four-in-One," because it is shared by four ethnic groups who have returned to Jerusalem from the Diaspora. When we arrived, Turkish tailors from Istanbul were about to hold a havdalah service to mark the departure of the *Shabbat Malkah,* the Sabbath Queen. The tailors were overjoyed when our group entered, because with the addition of our three men, there was a minyan, and God could be acceptably praised. No matter that none of our men knew how to read Hebrew, knew any of the prayers, knew, for that matter, what havdalah meant. They were three bodies complete with a penis apiece. They would suffice.

The four women in the group, two of whom did read Hebrew, did know the prayers, did understand havdalah, were sent upstairs to the *Ezrat Nashim,* the women's section, from which, behind a grille, we looked down at the male worshippers below. The synagogue was exotic, oriental: the wrought-iron bima, the altar surmounted with swirling columns like a church baldacchino, the double-doored ark of gilded and painted wood, the domed glass windows, the Persian carpet spread before the altar. We listened from on high as the tailors intoned the prayers in unfamiliar Eastern melodies. When the service was concluded, wine was passed around downstairs, and sprigs of sweet-smelling lemon verbena were distributed downstairs, tokens for a sweet week ahead.

The onlooking women would presumably have to provide their own week's sweetness.

A dark little girl stood down on the floor with her father before the ark. She darted around the men as they passed first the wine and then the sweet herbs, and suddenly, memory stabbed me and I wanted to cry out to her, Beware!

They will break your heart.

I did not, of course. When we three women tourists, and our female tour guide, descended the stairs, she and her father had already vanished into the evening shadows of weekday Jerusalem.

Rosh Hashanah and Yom Kippur came to mean pretty new clothes, and hats and gloves, and peer in the mirror one more time, how do I look? Very pretty. We trade our freedom for pretty clothes, for furs and silks and jewels, we end up frivolous and unfree. Men's clothing is more sensible, more suitable for moving around freely, for adventures. Women's clothing, however beautiful, is an encumbrance. Boys leave and travel and have adventures; girls stay home, looking pretty, and hear about them.

By New Year's, 1947, then, there were many new things in my life, a new school, a new baby sister, and a new freedom from the obligations of Jewish prayer life. By the time September rolled around, bringing another Rosh Hashanah and Yom Kippur, my dreams had turned from the radiance of Shekinah to the radiance of French fashion designer Christian Dior, who had just burst like a meteor upon our world, and his radiance penetrated even so far as Brooklyn.

It was 1947, the Year of the New Look.

A Cup of Blood

CHRISTIAN DIOR, INFANT PRODIGY of the fashion world, presented his first collection in February 1947, and in the twinkling of an eye all was changed. Women were utterly changed.

Dior took broad-shouldered, short-skirted, manfully straightforward wartime dames, and transformed them into upturned flowers.

His phrase.

Shoulders sloped, waists nipped in, skirts spread wide and full over layers of crinolines. Wartime austerity was dead at a single stroke, and women were suddenly seductive, yielding, tender, willowy.

Feminine.

In the bedroom I shared with my sister in Brooklyn I stared in the mirror and yearned to be transformed into an upturned flower. A lily, for preference.

And what did the mirror reflect back to me?

A small face, big ears, wide mouth, smallish hazel eyes, dirty blond hair in pigtails, an awkward gawky body, twelve and a half years old, no longer a little girl, emphatically not yet a woman, an ugly duckling.

With no guarantees on upcoming swandom, either.

The dream of my heart was to be beautiful. Well, I wasn't. Nor was I really ugly, either.

I was simply *plain*.

When would it happen, that magical day when I, too, would look in the mirror and see—

An upturned flower.

Obviously, not yet.

But things were speeding up, if not in my mirror, at least all around me.

At junior high, we were moving into high gear, more work, less time to do it in. Homework filled our evening hours, and began to invade our afternoon play time.

Our afternoon games were changing, anyway.

We girls didn't bounce balls any more, or play potsy, or roller-skate on the street. Now we took the subway to Flatbush, to a real indoor rink and wore shoe-skates and roller-skated to music, just like dancing, and looked at boys and dreamed of skating with them, arms linked, two bodies in perfect harmony, gliding around the rink, which was how, someday, you'd glide through life with your perfect partner.

We began taking long bike rides, to Coney Island and Plum Beach and Sheepshead Bay. We went by bus and streetcar and subway even farther from home, to Kings Highway, even to downtown Brooklyn, to the big movie theaters, to the gigantic Brooklyn Public Library at Grand Army Plaza, to Prospect Park for picnics and rock-climbing and visits to the zoo. Sometimes we would be a mixed group of boys and girls, which was fun but not really romantic, because we were all friends together, the same friends who had played unisex street games for years. These new games—joking, exploring, traveling, eating— were only more mature versions of the games we had always played in the afternoons.

In the evenings, though, we began experimenting with really new games. Sometimes, on Saturday nights, under the oblivious noses of our parents, in one finished basement or another (those being days before dens or family rooms), we played "kissing games": spin the bottle, post office. Greatly daring, pairing off briefly at the bottle's pointing, or the postman's summons.

I don't know how the other kids felt about these new games. I was a tumult of emotion, of desire and dread and shyness and anxiety all jumbled together, worried about what to do with my glasses, where to place my nose in a kiss, dreading being a dead letter, wanting, fearing.

It seems remote beyond belief, the kind of innocence even the most sophisticated of us brought to our new games. But there was no television, no unbridled advertising, no *Playboys* or *Playgirls*, even married couples inhabited separate beds in the movies. What did we know? Most of us were oldest children, so we didn't even have access to the wisdom of older teenagers. We were sheltered.

But we had bodies, and we had hormones, and they began teaching us, however little we understood of the process.

And there were other ways we learned about the differences between men and women.

Language teachers, for instance, were usually women, and hygiene teachers, and since physical education was segregated, girls were always taught by women in gym class. But science and math and social studies, *serious* subjects, were always taught by men.

There were movies, too, and novels, and what we gleaned from our parents, and there was, of course, the teaching of the synagogue where, one by one, the boys in our crowd were called up to the Torah, were bar mitzvah (not today's orgies of food and flowers and big bands, but simpler ceremonies ending with honey cake or sponge cake and wine), received a tallith and became part of the adult community of Jewish men; while as we girls turned thirteen, we passed a secular milestone whose significance was that we were becoming *teenagers,* no longer babies or little kids, but a genre apart.

Teenage girls.

Who turn, naturally, we upturned flowers, for our energy and warmth toward the sons.

Puns pack a lot of meaning in a small compass. Two little words, two punning homonyms, there it is.

SON/SUN

Lords of the universe.

And didn't I know it all along?

Adon Olam, Lord of the Universe, *Asher Malach,* who reigns as king. Male voices ringing out in the synagogue, *Adon Olam,* the lords of this earth saluting the Lord of the Universe, in whose image they were made.

And from the sidelines the women sang to praise their Lord and Master, whose image they serve on this earth.

For a while daughters could sit front and center with their fathers in the synagogue. But inexorably the day came for all of us when we too had to move to the sidelines, where our mothers sat.

As above, so below, in sacred matters and in secular, it was the same. The school mirrored the synagogue. And even among ourselves there was a turning.

Take the matter of The Club.

Sometime in the summer of 1946 the bunch of girls who'd played street games together decided, as befit *junior high students,* to have something more formal, more impressive. And so we established The Club, which had meeting days and dues and formal agendas and membership requirements. There were eight or so of us. What was our Club for anyway? Well, we gossiped about all the people we knew, and we experimented with Tangee lipstick, and talked about bras and underwear.

In our second year, however, a subtle shift became observable.

We began to become occupied with BOYS.

Now, when we gossiped, it was about the boys. Who do you like? Does he like you back? Does he like her instead? Whose side are you on? What do you say? What do you do? How do you look? Who do you become, if you want to please and flatter those demanding and capricious creatures who were our new magnetic North, the boys. Because it was firm Brooklyn Jewish women's folk wisdom that boys, like men, need to be pleased and propitiated and flattered.

No longer were we our own centers. We revolved around others, around The Boys, the sons became our suns.

But weren't these new suns the same boys we'd known all our lives, the ones we'd played games with, pushed and shoved and argued and laughed with forever, or so it seemed? What was so special about them all of a sudden that we deferred to them, thought and gossiped and schemed and daydreamed and planned about them?

What had happened to us?

No one else seemed to wonder about these things, though.

So perhaps the truth is that this new turning troubled me because I wasn't good at the new games. The new game was called Being Popular. I felt like I never knew the rules or, if I did catch on to one or two, suddenly, without warning, they'd be changed, and there'd be *newer* new rules.

Which I also wouldn't understand.

Oh, I had crushes, like everyone else, on Donald with the smooth yellow hair, and Saul, the craggy hall monitor in school, and Mr. Miletznick, the gentle joking science teacher, and Pistol Pete Reiser, the right fielder for the Brooklyn Dodgers.

But my *real* fantasy was not about *boys*. It was set in Ciudad Trujillo, where the Brooklyn Dodgers had their spring training camp, and where, every night, lying in my bed, I imagined playing shortstop for the Dodgers, their most brilliant rookie discovery, the only girl ever to play baseball in the major leagues, my secret fantasy, that I could share with no one.

Months wore on, months for me of tension, contradiction, ambiguity.

Christian Dior was calling upon us to be upturned flowers.

Squint as I might, I could not trace a flowery face and form in the mirror.

And yet I wasn't any longer the same, either.

I was, in the phrase of the day, *developing*.

My breasts were budding and beginning to ripen. Downy blond hair thickened on my arms, sprouted in my armpits, coarsened on my legs, to my mingled shame and gratification.

My friend Sheila began to mutter mysteriously about things to come.

You know, she would whisper darkly. *Periods*.

What on earth was she talking about?

Periods were punctuation marks, dots at the end of sentences. What on earth was she talking about *dots* for?

But she would never explain, just smile in a maddening, superior kind of way.

You'll find out.

Summer ended, school began again, my thirteenth birthday came and went untroubled by ritual entry into the covenant of the Jewish people.

What did the covenant have to do with me?

My membership was in The Club.

Fall waned, while my yearning to be beautiful, to be glamorous, to be loved increased in intensity. But every night before I went to sleep I still solaced myself by playing shortstop for the Brooklyn Dodgers.

The year 1947 went out with a near-blizzard, and 1948 entered with a full-scale blizzard followed by freak fogs. In early spring, devastating tornadoes spun across the American landscape. And on Tuesday, March 9, 1948, my own personal landscape was altered irrevocably by an issue of blood.

I went to the bathroom that afternoon, and as I wiped myself I found blood on the toilet paper, and there was blood in the toilet bowl.

Not very much, dark red, not very bright. But it was blood.

Did I know what it was about?

I knew that *something* was happening, something that was supposed to happen, but without any real understanding. And so—because it is an appropriate response to a mysterious happening—I was afraid.

And, afraid, I went downstairs to tell my mother.

Who slapped me across the face.

Nothing personal, as it were.

The slap in the face is the time-honored traditional response of Jewish mothers (maybe other kinds of mothers, for all I know) to the physical entry of their daughters into the covenant of womanhood.

They're *supposed* to slap you in the face.

I don't know why; neither did my mother.

That's what you did, that's all. It was a tradition.

My mother told me, in the traditional way, that now I was a woman because I had my period.

My period!

She brought me to the store and bought me a sanitary belt and a box of Kotex sanitary napkins. Kotex also put out a booklet, offered on the box, explaining the process of menstruation. I think it was called "What Every Young Girl Should Know." My mother told me to send for that.

And then she went back to the kitchen.

And that was it for sex education in the home.

My first diary entry, March 9, reads (in its entirety), I started to menstruate. Thursday's entry: I'm still menstruating. Those were probably the first and last times I used the dictionary word.

Normally, we had our periods.

Or we had fallen off the roof, or we were wearing the rag, or, delicately, it was our time of the month. But before many months had passed, I, like the others, used our name of choice.

Are you going to gym today?

No, I have the curse.

In Deuteronomy God says to the people through Moses: "Behold, I set before you this day life and death, the blessing and the curse; therefore choose life, that you may live."

Choose the blessing, says God. Not the curse.

I didn't know about that injunction then.

And I never *chose* anything, either.

This monthly issue of blood familiarly known as the curse was thrust upon me.

Menstrual flow is not just any old blood, like cutting your finger. It is the disintegration of the lining of the uterus prepared every month within normal women of childbearing age, beginning roughly between twelve or thirteen years, and ending anywhere from forty to sixty years. Every lunar month, hormones trigger the preparation of a nesting place in the uterus, a thick soft dark nourishing carpet into which a fertilized egg can snuggle down for a cozy nine-month gestation; which is why menstrual periods stop during pregnancy, because the rich lining of nutrients is being utilized. But if an egg is not met and penetrated by an adequate sperm, then the egg continues on its downward journey and eventually, unnoticed, or at most marked by a single spot of blood, is pissed away. Then the uterine lining, so carefully fashioned to nourish and to cherish, is abandoned by the body, and excreted, sometimes easily, often with cramps and clots and near-hemorrhage. Mother Nature, an unsentimental bitch, knows there is always next month.

And that is how human life is perpetuated on our planet.

So why a curse? Why not a blessing?

Of all the many names, colloquial and scientific, for the phenomenon of menstruation, none of them is Blessing.

We're talking about *blood* now.

We're talking about the vigor of young bloods, in the prime of their manhood. And about the intimacy of blood brothers. And the closest of bonds: you are my own flesh and blood.

We are talking about battlefields, like Flanders or Gettysburg, sacred by virtue of the blood which was spilled there, the sweetest of sacrifices, is it not? To spill one's blood for one's country, so sweet and so sacred that it hallows the very ground which drinks up the blood.

Blood of heroes.

Blood of martyrs, the food of the church.

And we are talking about the solemn and sacred sacrifice of the Mass, in which the priest, in the consecration, presides over the transsubstantiation of wafer and wine, so that the actual salvific body and blood of Jesus Christ becomes present, to be consumed by his people, who are thereby hallowed, so sweet and so efficacious was his sacrifice.

Because the blood is the *life*.

That's the point.

Blood is not death.

The blood is the life, the body's vital fluid, the source of our vitality.

That is why, in order to make meat *kosher,* that is, *clean,* for Jewish consumption, it must be kashered. The meat is placed on a board, salted, and left to stand for a fixed period until the blood rises to the surface and is drained off down the sink. Jewish meat is always well-done, because the blood has already been drained off; and it would seem to be clear, at least to me, that the reason is the sacredness of the blood, so sacred that it is not fitting to be consumed by us.

The blood belongs to God.

This is a Christian, certainly a Catholic, understanding as well.

The incarnation of Jesus as a human being of flesh and blood redeemed the flesh from its stigma of baseness, and Christians were redeemed from death to life in his blood. (Or so was the intention.)

The blood of Christ, the living sacrifice.

It poured from his side, mingled blood and water, at the thrust of a spear into the crucified flesh of this young Jewish man.

There is even a hymn about it:

> *Rock of Ages, cleft for me,*
> *Let me hide myself in thee.*
> *Let the water and the blood*
> *From thy wounded side that flowed,*
> *Be of sin the double cure.*

But that is surely a feminine image, isn't it?

Who is cleft?

And who is the hiding place?

Who is the receptacle and the comforter?

Who sheds the water and the blood?

Didn't anyone ever notice the femininity of Jesus as he hung helpless on the cross, pierced by a soldier's spear thrust, spilling his water and blood?

Biologically women are a nation of priests, a holy gender. Male priests of the temple have to kill to get the blood to offer to God. Their sacrifices mean certain death, death to attain new life.

Women shed their own blood, sacrifice themselves, in the service of new life. Mother and developing child share one bloodstream. The child is washed in the blood of the mother, children are not blood of their fathers, but of their mothers.

All blood is sacred and hallowing, except in one form.

Women's menstrual flow of blood makes them unclean.

That holds true in Judaism and in Catholicism, the two religions I know intimately; it may well be true of many, or all religions.

In Orthodox Judaism, a menstruating woman is banned every month from the company of men. She may eat at the same table as her husband, but she is not to hand him anything, lest she defile him by her touch. She must not sleep in the same bed with him. And when the days of her period are finished, she is still unclean until she goes to the ritual bath, the *mikveh,* and, after elaborate preparation and prayer, she is immersed from toes to top of head, to wash away the uncleanness.

After bloody childbearing, in which a woman labors long and hard to bring forth new life, obeying the injunction of God to be fruitful, she is unclean for seven days if she has a son, fourteen if she has a daughter, and then she must be purified again in the mikveh before she is fit to touch the hem of her husband's garment.

That same practice obtained in the Catholic church for centuries, until recently. It was called churching. After a woman had given birth, she had to wait a set time before she could return to church, and when she did, she could not enter rejoicing, bearing her sheaves of wheat. She had to wait outside the church, a supplicant, until the priest came to lead her in. But her touch defiled, just as in Judaism, so the priest offered her an end of his stole to hold, and thus she was led in, at arm's length, to be cleansed and made fit for the company of her Christian community.

Criminals could demand sanctuary with less fuss.

I would rather think that if women are not to be touched during these times of issue of blood, it is because they are consecrated, holy, set apart for God.

Honored. Blessed.

Instead, we are cursed.

Slapped across the face. Now you are a woman.

I was, through no fault or option of my own, unclean. And cursed. That marked a profound turning in my spiritual life.

What does menstruation have to do with God?

Plenty.

The extent and the nature of the way in which you are alienated from other humans is the same extent and nature of the way in which you're alienated from God.

So menstruation brings me to the War Between Men and Women, the war in which, because of my gender, my entry into the covenant and the army of women, I had just been decisively recruited; and so menstruation also determined my relationship with a male God who followed the Enemy Way, who expelled me from the heart of his house of worship, who pointed his finger at me, Unclean. One had to be as wary, then, of this God as of the men created in his image. No trust, no forgiveness, only vigilance.

Be eternally on guard.

This is the way of the world, then: men get the blessing, women get the curse, and that's the way it is. Who would want to be a woman?

I was nearly torn apart by ambivalence. I wanted to be a woman, I was unready and unwilling to be one. I wanted to seek and be sought out by men, I wanted to flee from men. The War Between Men and Women had shifted to my own psyche, and I became my own battle-field. The masculine and feminine principles within me, the yin and the yang, instead of harmonizing, tugged fiercely at each other.

With the onset of menstruation I let go of my twilight fantasies about playing shortstop for the Brooklyn Dodgers. Girls could fantasize so, but not women.

What price upturned flowers?

The fall term flew by. The boys founded their own club, named it

The Jesters, and bought club jackets, the kind we now associate with street gangs. One faction of our own Club wanted to get matching jackets designating us the Jesterettes. My faction was all for jackets, but balked at becoming a ladies' auxiliary, wanted to keep our own club name. The division between us was so sharp, the arguments so bitter, that our Club foundered on this rock of identity, splintered, and sank without trace. Within days The Club was as if it had never existed, as if there had never been a time when we were all girls together.

And then we were truly no longer all girls together in any way. With three children in it, our house was now too small for our family, so we found another out on Long Island. My Brooklyn classmates and I graduated from Cunningham Junior High School, but while they entered long-anticipated James Madison High School, I set off, a pioneer, to the exotic, mysterious, far-off suburb of Great Neck.

Set off, like my Texas mother coming, a pioneer, to the East; and ended up, just as she had, an exile.

A World with Christians in It

M Y MOTHER LIKED JEWELRY. She had a lot of it, both real and costume, but to my sister and me, who loved to play with it, all of it was real. And beautiful.

Topaz was my birthstone. It wasn't really gaudy enough for me, though. Insipid yellow, I thought it. Sapphires, deep blue sapphires, were mine, because I was fair, just as rich red rubies suited my dark sister. In our play we divided up my mother's articulated bangles of colored stones and diamonds. The sapphire bangle would be mine, and the ruby, my sister's. We loved to hold them and look at them and wear them, pretending we were grown-up, pretending we were glamorous, like my mother.

It turned out that they weren't diamond-and-sapphire at all. Or diamond-and-ruby.

They were only a good imitation.

I loved gold and jewels.

Why not?

What could be more appropriate to show forth the splendor of God?

God's beauty.

Because God is in beautiful things. They image him, reveal him.

That was my childhood impulse: one of the faces by which God reveals himself to us is Beauty.

Which also tells us something about the nature of God: that he gives freely.

If you stop to think about it, beauty is pure gift. It isn't *good* for anything.

It isn't *useful*.

It's only—beautiful.

It serves nothing more nor less than our delight and our pleasure. It pleases God to delight us, to please us. You don't think so? Look at the world around you, the sky, a sunset, waves, the bark of a tree, the simplest shell, an onion. Really look.

I like things to look pretty.

I like the ordinary to be transformed, to be made sparkling, and special.

I wanted *me* to be transformed. I wanted the plain ordinary me to become dazzling.

Like a princess.

Who is, after all, only an ordinary girl, transformed.

My mother had a rhinestone bandeau, and, when I wore it in my hair to a costume party, I was transformed into a princess, at least for a while.

I was an imaginative, nervous, inward-turning, lonely child with, presumably, an inborn appetite for the world of wonders.

I loved spring, the tender green of crocuses peeping through barren ground, and bulbs blooming, purple and yellow and white of crocus, yellow daffodils, red tulips emerging from nothing, from nowhere, from the dead earth, magically. A yearly miracle.

And I liked summer, when green leaves unfurled and cast a deep green shade, and days lasted so long that I could play outside to my heart's content and still be in bed before darkness fully overtook the world.

I loved fall, crisp air and hectic colors, red and orange and yellow, like fire, and then the pleasure of scuffing through heaps of dry leaves, making them fly in the air one last time.

Then came November, when the last of the leaves fluttered to the ground, and the bare bones of the trees, their skeletons, were revealed as what they have always been—bare, naked, forked, unaccommodated.

And then December arrived, and that was the most magical season of all.

I remember winter as a wonderland. It brought snow, and ice, and Christmas.

Now Christmas meant almost nothing to me when I was growing up. It's important to understand that, just as Christianity had almost no meaning.

I lived in a Jewish world. The word for "others," for those who were different from us, who were not Jewish, was *goyim*.

Gentiles. Other people.

A Hottentot black from the African sun was a *goy,* just as the Italian fruit vendor with his funny accent was a *goy*.

They were simply *not Jewish*. Not Christian, nor heathen, nor anything else. Just not Jewish.

Mine was a Jewish world.

All I knew of Christianity came in the mail, in Christmas cards and Christmas catalogs.

The Christmas cards that arrived at our house were from my father's non-Jewish clients. They showed Dickensian coaching scenes, or snow-covered cottages nestled in evergreen forests, or wreaths of holly, or deer, or birds. But whatever the picture, the cards were all lavishly dusted with some snowy substance, a glitter unlike the kind we know now, a glitter that really looked like snow, like new-fallen snow, which always sparkled in the lamplight and delighted my eyes.

The sparkle of those cards to me was everything that was shining, and mysterious, and promising.

The Christmas catalogs we got, from Macy's and from Abraham & Straus, paltry affairs by today's standards, were still more shining promises of beauty.

That, if anything, was Christmas.

It seems to be a widespread myth that every Jewish child envies Christian children their Christmas trees, their presents.

But I didn't. Not as a young child, certainly.

I didn't really even *see* many Christmas trees. We shopped mostly at Jewish stores, so the amount of tinsel garlands and decoration to which I was exposed was minimal. I had no Christian friends' trees or presents to covet. And, of course, in those days there was no such thing as television.

But why would I need Christmas anyway?

I had Chanukah.

Back in the old days, before merchandising transformed Chanukah into a buying orgy of alternate Christmas, Chanukah wasn't a rival of anything. It was what it was, a celebration of bravery, of the bravery of the Maccabees, that band of heroic brothers who had liberated our holy Temple from the Romans; and it was a celebration of the cleaning of the desecrated holy place and the rekindling of the eight-branched candelabrum burning there to the glory of God; and it was a memorial to the miracle that was wrought there, when only enough oil remained to keep the lamps burning for a single day, and it would take the fastest runners eight days to bring a fresh supply of oil, but God wrought his miracle! Behold, the lamps burned for eight whole days on that one little mite of oil, and the flame, relit, did not go out again.

(Nor ever again, so far as I internalized the story, although historically, it was, how long—fifty years? less?—before the light went out forever, and the Romans destroyed the Temple after all, laid it waste, in ruins, as it remains to this day, although the rest of rebuilt Jerusalem rises glorious around its site. And Jews still weep and wail before the ruined remnant, the Wall which is the only remaining artifact, and a remainder only of the outer protecting wall at that, not even a wall of the Temple itself; and a mosque stands atop the Temple Mount, and internecine massacres, of spirit, sometimes of flesh, are continually reenacted, and hatred is alive and well between these brothers, no Maccabees they. Or all Maccabees.)

Were the Maccabees heroes or fanatics? Both? Neither? This is a complex world we live in. Only to a child are things so simple.

But Chanukah to me was not politics.

It was candles, orange candles, burning bravely in the eight-armed menorah, lit in dramatic order, one on the first night, two on the second, and so on, until on the eighth night there was a satisfying blaze to commemorate and celebrate those brave Jewish brothers, and God's miracle for the Jewish people. And we marked it by singing, *Ma-oz Tzur*, "Rock of Ages," and we spun little tops called dreidels, and we got presents *every night* for eight nights. Oh, we didn't get big presents, or expensive ones. We'd get fancy pencils, barrettes, paper dolls. But they were surprises, night after night, eight nights, and we were thrilled by them.

So much for Christmas! If I spared any thought at all for non-Jewish children, it was to pity them, that *they* didn't get presents for eight nights, only for one.

So part of the shock I received when we moved to Great Neck was the discovery of a world with Christians in it.

Great Neck was not, in those days, the overgrown city-suburb it is today. Now it is famous, one of the wealthiest Jewish communities in the nation, high-styled, high-powered, fast-moving.

Back then, Great Neck was a small town. It had a larger Jewish population than most Long Island communities. My parents wouldn't have moved there, for instance, if a Conservative congregation hadn't already been in existence for my father to attend every week. And there was also a kosher butcher, to round out the town's Jewish quali-fications.

But the bulk of the population was certainly Christian, with the tone set by the WASP majority. An *Episcopalian* tone. Great Neck was still essentially old money and old values: understatement, quiet wealth *never* to be flaunted, good taste, good manners. Upper-middle-class entitlement that frowns on grabbing because, of course, it doesn't have to. It already *has*.

It's important that you know that Great Neck was snobbish. Not about anything so crude or straightforward as money.

It was more a snobbery of style, of *belonging*.

A far cry, all this tastefulness, from restless, impatient, thrusting immigrant peoples, whether Jews from the Lower East Side, or Irish or Italian Catholics from Manhattan's West Side or Little Italy. The prevailing atmosphere for the sons and daughters of Jewish and Irish and Italian immigrants was set by the elder daughters of the Junior League and the Women's Club.

Great Neck was conservative, traditional, small-town America. Not exactly Norman Rockwell, mind you. But not so far removed.

In those days Great Neck even *looked* like a Norman Rockwell. There were white spired churches, and strong stone churches, one of which was actually the Reform temple, Temple Beth-El. There were broad tree-lined streets and rolling lawns and great pillared mansions and gracious verandah-wrapped frame houses. The high school was red brick, with white neo-Greek columns, and might have served as a set for an Andy Hardy movie. Small-town America.

The school was small, too. My graduating class was scarcely over 250. At that time, Great Neck's population had been remarkably stable, which meant that my new school contained a solid front of teenagers, most of whom had known one another since kindergarten.

Clique was the word used in those days to describe such tight-knit groups. Great Neck teenagers were actually not so monolithic as I supposed; there were cliques within cliques, but it took me quite some time to figure that out.

They seemed a united front.

Impregnable.

And I?

Invisible.

I don't remember anyone's being directly rude or nasty or mean to me in those early days.

Why should they be? I simply didn't exist. I was invisible.

Fourteen is a tough age anyway—uncertain, transformative, insecure; and for those reasons, cruel.

But in Brooklyn I had always been an *insider.*

In Great Neck, I was suddenly and completely *outside.*

That first year or so in Great Neck was, simply, hell. I was used to being lonely at home. My social world had been primarily school and friends. In Great Neck, my loneliness became unrelieved and unrelenting, all the time, everywhere. It entered my bones.

Loneliness meant no one to walk to school with, to walk home with. Loneliness meant no one to sit with at lunch, no one to gossip or giggle with at free time, no one to hail in the halls. Loneliness meant no one to telephone in the evenings, to talk over homework with, no one to go to the movies with, or to a party with on weekends.

Like Mormon shunning.

The loneliness and alienation of adolescence is hardly uncommon, so to some degree what I'm describing is nothing extraordinary.

The really damaging aspect of this sudden exile were the conclusions I drew from it, global conclusions that redefined me for myself so thoroughly that for years and years, well into mature womanhood, whatever my actual social situation, my responses, feelings, and perceptions were those of an outsider.

An undesirable, someone *less than.*

Do you want to know the truth? Sometimes I still feel like that.

There's a kind of a corollary to that first conclusion: the most important thing in the world, far more important than being *me* and expressing that real undesirable self, the most important thing in the world was to *belong.* To be like everybody else. To fit in. However impossible it seemed to achieve, that became my goal.

That wasn't necessity. I didn't have to have drawn that particular conclusion. It was a choice, but a choice made in ignorance and un-awareness and pain, as disastrous as most choices made in similar cir-cumstances. But for thirty-five years or so, I simply accepted the consequences of those decisions as "the way things are."

I would have sold my soul to belong, to be one of the group, just like everyone else. My problem was that I didn't know how to do it, to whom to offer my soul.

And that is how the unease of my final years in Brooklyn—when my friends began to play new games with rules I didn't know, when popularity had replaced anything else as a sole goal and value—be-came, in Great Neck, my way of life.

My social alienation at school was mirrored in my alienation at temple. Same kids, of course.

Most Jewish freshmen were already part of an ongoing confirma-tion class either at the Reform temple or the Conservative temple. With tutoring I could have caught up with them, but my parents wouldn't hear of it.

You see, the real distinction made in my home, and if truth be told, in many if not most Jewish homes, is *not* between Jew and Christian. It is between Jew and goy. Christian, Hindu, Buddhist, all equally goyim. And confirmation was considered *goyish.*

Now goyim doesn't mean *bad,* exactly. I mean, just because you're a goy doesn't make you bad. You can be very nice, in fact. But being a goy does make you a little bit less than. A little unlucky, that you weren't born Jewish.

I fervently recited the *Shema,* the central Jewish affirmation: *Shema Yisroel, Adonai Elohenu, Adonai Echod.*

Hear, O Israel, the Lord is our God, the Lord is One.

But what that meant to me was subtly different.

The Lord is our God.

Ours.

Not necessarily yours.

I suppose what I believed actually was: Yes, there's one *real* God. And we've got him.

There were lots of false gods, I knew that. Jesus, for one, and Mohammed, and all those statues in India and China and heathen places—

I guess I thought everybody except Jews were heathens. I didn't condemn anybody for being a heathen. It was just their *mazel,* their luck, or lack of it, that they weren't born into the Chosen People.

And the only legitimate ceremony for a Jewish child was bar mitzvah, to be called up to read from the Torah and the Haftorah before the entire congregation, and to be received as an adult member of the community. Unfortunately, even in Reform or Conservative temples, in those days there was no such thing as a bat mitzvah, the same ceremony, but for a girl. It was only for boys. So, in the world of the temple, as in the school world, there was no place for me, neither confirmation nor bar mitzvah.

I stood outside. Other.

But otherness, in the event, was what pulled me through.

In my Great Neck High School yearbooks there are inscriptions in Spanish, German, French, Greek, Chinese. The names are extraordinarily varied, foreign names that I roll on my tongue like poetry: Alex Contostavlos, Nina de Lozada, Malda Hammersla, Milan Kerno, Yuan Chang, Urania Liu, Tassilo von Schmidt Pauli.

The fledgling United Nations was then headquartered at Lake Success, which is a part of Great Neck; and many of these exotic names belonged to diplomats' children. Furthermore, coming from a strictly homogeneous Jewish neighborhood, names like MacAleer, Murphy, Brown, Hallenbeck, Wessel, Nelson, Dorsey, and Larrabee were equally exotic to me. In the beginning they were all equally *other.* I found that world with "others" in it very attractive, and more welcoming than the Great Neck Jewish world.

As time wore on, however, I also became aware of the diversity that had been invisible to me at the beginning.

That solid unanimous front, all kids together, had chinks in it through which I too could enter. I never became a part of the crowd of the most popular Jewish girls, the best-dressed, the style setters. But there were other Jewish kids, boys and girls, more intellectually or politically inclined, with whom I felt some kinship, and there were all kinds of others whose interests were wider still.

I danced my way into belonging, in a manner of speaking. Modern dance was a popular high school activity for girls. Afterschool dance cut across all lines of grade, religion, and clique. In dance rehearsals, in recitals, it was once again as it had been in jump-rope days, *All in together, girls.*

I was okay in dance, good enough to dance solo in several recitals, which restored a little of my vanished self-esteem. Some girls whom I met in sophomore year through the expediency of car pools also liked to dance, and we became friends as we danced together.

Those were good times.

In junior year I joined the high school choir. In kindergarten I had been labeled a listener for "Silent Night." But our high school A Cappella Choir turned no one away. They were even happy to have a deep alto. The choir was expected to be the backbone of the annual community *Messiah* sing-in, when what seemed like all Great Neck brought along musical scores and thundered Hallelujahs to the rafters of the high school auditorium, a community making music together.

What was the effect on me of participating in those sacred texts, that soaring music? Now I know that it had seminal effect. But subliminally. The *Messiah* was goyish, after all. Those thundering Hallelujahs had nothing to do with the *real* God who lived in synagogues and spoke Hebrew.

Who knew that Hallelujah *was* Hebrew?

Or that it was a word for all people?

Not me.

In Great Neck some of us Jewish kids went out caroling on Christmas Eve, to serenade our Christian friends and neighbors and to end up with hot chocolate and doughnuts at somebody's house. Those frosty starry nights, a bunch of us wandering the streets, brought to life for me long-ago Christmas cards dusted with snowy glitter that I had loved so much as a child.

I didn't belong to Christmas, it's true. I was Jewish, but I belonged to the carolers, and that was enough.

The world was bigger than I had thought, wider, different.

Through dance, through music, through song, I belonged in the world.

A Lawyer's Daughter, and a
Day in the Country

A LL WASN'T LOST FOR ME at Great Neck High School, because of one talent with which I was born.

I am a good student.

That's a genetic attribute, I think, like the natural balance of an athlete, or the perfect pitch of a musician. Not a talent to take credit for, only one to polish or to neglect.

I usually ended up with A's in every subject, but all subjects weren't equal for me. Take math, for instance. I always had to work hard in math, relying on memorization rather than understanding. Science was better, a little more interesting than math, but I had little patience for detailed methodology, and I had to work pretty hard to keep my grades high. I never went on to physics, because there was too much math in it. Anyway, physics was for boys, anybody knew *that*.

On the other hand, languages, first Spanish, then Latin, came so easily and naturally to me they were like breathing. I never minded working at them. They were interesting. And even back then I think I already glimpsed the truth that every language has its own genius, its own presiding spirit, that, from the standpoint of sound, connotation, nuance, and structural relationship, you can say a particular kind of thing better in one language than in another. But I enjoyed languages most because they were for talking, and I was a talker, a chatterbox. My parents said I'd talked from the day I was born, so naturally I loved languages. And I loved English best of all.

Even though some of my English teachers managed to make their subject matter boring, others touched my life and altered it.

There was, in my junior year, a feisty, vital, loving redheaded lady in early middle age. I don't know which was her most important act of loving: her love of the English language, or her love of life, or her love of her students. Maybe the three were inseparable for her, so that there was a Trinitarian wholeness, a three-in-one, in her that drew love, certainly my love, in return.

She read poetry well, and stories too. She spoke interestingly, criticized only with encouragement. Sparks flew from her, from her blue eyes, from her quick words. And her words were quickest—isn't it remarkable what we remember as important?—every time someone sneezed in class. She would stop in the middle of her sentence and, without pausing, would intone in a single breath: Godblessyouand-keepyouandprotectyoufromthedangersofthisworldAmen. One word, one thought, one blessing. And without a break, she would go on and finish her original sentence.

Every time.

Not gabbled. She didn't gabble it, she *said* it, quickly but deliberately, with intention, because a benediction was needed, and she could invoke it.

There's white magic for you.

It wasn't magic, either. I don't know how, but I knew with certainty that I was in the presence of one who really believed and loved and worshipped a God who protected children.

Not so long ago I spoke to her again, an old lady, her voice still vibrant, her enthusiasm crackling over the phone wire. Why, yes, she was a believer, devout, practicing. Yes, she loved her church, loved her faith, loved God. Not soppily. She was never a sentimental Irish-woman. She was bracing, she was astringent, she was funny.

And loving. A lovely lady.

In senior year I chose creative writing as my English elective. I had already done a great deal of what I thought of as "public" writing, on the high school newspaper—objective, timely writing, what in years to come would be called *relevant*. Realistic, rhetorical, detached, *serious* writing.

Now I had an opportunity to explore the realm of "private" writing. Our class was taught by a short, thin, prematurely balding man with glasses like goggles, who was an insignificant physical presence, odd-looking even.

He was another who loved literature, language, words, a wonderful teacher, inspired and inspiring. Above all, he loved his students. He made us feel special.

He encouraged us to try on all kinds of faces and voices, to experi-ment, explore, imagine, play with words. To *enjoy* them.

Private writing, in my mind, was subjective, fanciful, imaginative, whimsical, engaged. It was not "cool"; it was hot, passionate, emotional. Frivolous, I suppose I judged it to be. Which is a pejo-rative word, and ultimately that patronizing nuance is the one I ac-cepted.

But not yet. Not during that semester of exploration, when we wrote a little fiction, some description, some character sketches, and lots and lots of poetry. I discovered in this private writing that I could exorcise demons, expel devils of anger, jealousy, fear, loneliness, lust, chase them onto pages of buff typing paper, objectify them, skewer them in print, and thereby ease my overburdened teenage heart. I discovered that it was possible to use writing as a means of revenge, or to make people laugh.

What I wrote most, though, was love poetry, great quantities of it. I was "half in love with easeful Death," anyway, from the travails of teenage crushes and puppy love, so in verse I wallowed in moping and moaning and delightful misery. My poetry was mostly melancholy, filled with gloom and sorrow, and heavily sprinkled with *doths* and *dosts,* derived mostly from Elizabethan lyrics.

Some of these gloomy outpourings I thought were very rare and fine, so I copied them out carefully in white ink on colored composition paper and bound them myself into a little volume of which I was exceedingly proud, but which I showed to no one. My, my.

Despite the excess passion, I did very well in my English classes, so well that at graduation I received the prize for outstanding achievement in English. Even before that, "everyone," by whom I mean my parents and relatives, many of my teachers, and even some of my friends, assumed I would go on to become an English major in college and subsequently teach English in junior high or high school.

Wrong. Not for me.

The fact that they all were essentially right and *I* was wrong, is irrelevant. The choice I was making was not about studying English. It was about identity and autonomy. It was the place where I dug in my heels, said No, I will be who *I* will be, not who *you* think I should be. I wasted a lot of years of my life because of my rebelliousness, but it was then, for me, necessary.

What I had chosen instead of English was social studies, because, like math and science, it was a "hard" subject.

By my standard, "soft" subjects, English and language studies, for example, were subjective, emotional, irrational, essentially private, and therefore irrelevant in the larger world. They were frills, and frills were —well, feminine. Softheaded.

Like teaching, which I also considered *feminine.* Teaching was an acceptable, even desirable, occupation for women who had to work: you dealt with children, which was obviously suitable female work; you had good hours and ample vacations, which was an advantage if you married and had children yourself; and if you were unfortunate enough never to marry, well, you would have the status and respectability and security you would so sorely need.

Teaching was women's work.

No, what I respected were the hardheaded subjects: the tough-minded, statistical, objective, useful, pure and rational and logical studies, in short, what to me represented the *masculine*. The public world.

I had neither the aptitude nor the interest to compete in the worlds of math or science. But social studies was a different story.

Social studies was about history, past and present, and about the institutions and structures of the world outside the home, the public world. Above all, for me, it was about politics, and about law.

And I was a lawyer's daughter.

There it is, the single influence, stronger than loneliness, stronger than love, which determined the course of my high school and college education, and my career beyond that education.

I was a lawyer's daughter.

It was in the tenth grade that I really began to come into my own with my father on Friday nights and Saturday noons at our extended Sabbath meals. I was excited about the things I was learning in social studies. And my father responded to my excitement about history and politics and law with his own.

That was when the "word game" first began. We would get into an argument about the exact meaning of a word, its particular nuance, its subtle signification.

"I buy you a dictionary, you don't even use it. Go and look it up."

Thus, my father. It was the rare Sabbath meal that wasn't interrupted by my jumping up to consult *Webster's Unabridged* in the den, returning with six or eight possible meanings of a word, plus its etymology.

For a long time, my father was invariably right.

But then, inevitably, came the day, maybe toward the end of my junior year, when he was wrong and I was right.

There he was, caught between pride in his offspring and chagrin at his defeat.

Winning and losing was the mode of being in our household, just as it was in the courtroom.

You don't go to trial to play around. You go to win.

The dinner table was my training ground. There I learned to want to win, and the skills necessary to do so.

What did I learn?

How to narrate a story logically and sequentially. What necessary details to include, and how to omit irrelevancies. How to sift inferences from facts. To be precise in my language, accurate in my details, telling in my evidence.

Oh, it drove my father wild, the way my mother told a story, jumping in just anywhere, digressing constantly, leaving out material evidence, a hodgepodge of gossip and irrelevancies and inferences. Wild, it drove him!

I would learn differently.

And I did.

I yearned to please my father. And my mother did not.

Those attributes she displayed, the ones I despised and hated—the illogical, irrational, overemotional, superstitious, passive, sullen, withdrawing attributes—those were not simply a function of who she was. They were part of her weaponry in the War Between Men and Women.

She knew she drove my father wild when she told a story every which way. She would get exasperated at his questions and interruptions and flare up, or sullenly withdraw, and either way, look like the victim she was.

But only partly a victim. Partly she did it on purpose. Partly she was exercising her own brand of hostility and aggression, a passive aggression that passes for martyrdom and victimization.

I chose instead to go to my father for schooling, and I received a liberal education from him at the dinner table.

A valuable education.

Because surely those are valuable skills, to be able to think straight, to narrate clearly, accurately, concisely, coherently. Those skills have stood me in good stead all my life, for which I have to thank my father the lawyer.

But those same skills are tools perhaps too powerful for a fifteen- or sixteen-year-old with an intellect way ahead of her emotional grasp. Certainly too powerful for a girl in a society in which it was, perhaps still is, *unwomanly* to use too skillfully the masculine tools of reason and logic.

In my enthusiasm, I used those delicate sharp-edged tools as spears, as bludgeons, used them as weapons, to win, because that's what lawyers do, isn't it?

Intellectually my training was invaluable. Psychologically, things were trickier.

"Lawyerly" is more than a function in society. It is also a stance toward life, fueled by suspiciousness, cynicism, skepticism, and defensiveness. It thrives on a diet of adages: Do lest you be done to; Mistrust all; Expect the worst and be prepared for it; Catch out the other guy before he catches you.

To be a lawyer is to live on guard.

But the seamlessness of classroom and social life made things difficult to negotiate. An active and aggressive stance was a good thing for boys, and to be encouraged. That was clear.

But girls?

Girls were meant to be pliant, cooperative, helpful, sensitive to the needs of others, nurturing, soft, clinging, emotional, tender, responsive, selfless. Girls were to be listeners, not talkers; followers, not leaders.

How could I possibly reconcile this self-effacing, passive feminine philosophy with my passionate desire to be the hardheaded, forceful, aggressive, powerful thinker and achiever my father valued and admired?

The uncivil War Between Men and Women, now internalized, played itself out for me in the classroom: I would fight, no-holds-barred, in the simplest discussion. And usually win. But in the attitudes of my male classmates afterward, I felt the rebound. Every classroom victory was also a social defeat, and after each I would vow tearfully to myself that *next* time I would keep my mouth shut.

It was when my father the lawyer used this same adversarial stance for my social and sexual education that matters took a more serious turn.

My father was not merely an American lawyer, he was also a Talmudist, steeped in Jewish law and tradition. Certain legal concepts were therefore especially congenial to him, and chief among them was the Talmudic concept of the *hedge*. Mankind being what it is, to safeguard something by one single prohibition isn't enough. We are too weak, temptations are too strong. So one surrounds the original prohibition with an extra prohibition, a "hedge" or fence surrounding the forbidden tree in the garden, widening the protective circle.

My father taught an ineluctability of human desire, perceived as so intense that we humans are helpless to take free action against such an overwhelming force.

And the prime example of the attractive compulsion of evil is— woman.

My father did not invent his attitude toward women. He inherited it legitimately from a strain of Rabbinic Judaism which teaches that women, by their intrinsic nature, are seductresses. And destroyers, designed to ensnare the most virtuous of men, unless they are safeguarded by formidable hedges.

So Orthodox Jewish men practice what Catholic priests used to know as custody of the eyes, and they do not look at strange women, that is, any woman not their mother, wife, sister, or daughter. The hair of married Orthodox women, like that of nuns used to be, is cut off, because a woman's crowning glory is a net to trap men, and her husband's virtue, as well as her own, must be protected.

Oh, this teaching is usually disguised under a cloud of words like modesty, purity, cleanliness. But the real fear and intent is readily inferred from the number and nature of religious prohibitions, from custom, and from many Rabbinic *midrash,* teaching stories. And the jokes of stand-up Jewish comedians will also serve.

Although I was happy at being my father's best student, there was something unsatisfying to me about the misogynistic, negative, pessimistic, deterministic view of human nature I was being taught.

And then, too, I wonder: if women are such powerful, dark, and destructively overwhelming forces, what does that imply about men? That they are merely weak, driven creatures, moths fluttering to a flame? Or perhaps there is another explanation, the one which I absorbed. Men, driven by irresistible desire for women, become transformed into swine, ravening wild boars, tusks at the ready to thrust and pierce.

Men succumb to the fatal attraction of women's bodies and are no longer responsible or accountable for their behavior. They become beasts, and can't help themselves.

Sat in on any rape trials lately? This is no outmoded argument, but one as timely as today's headlines.

So, women, be on guard.

Thus my father's God, a God of law, my father his prophet.

The lawyer's stance: be on guard.

The War Between Men and Women had crystallized in my adolescent mind into a battle between the forces of light and logic and intellect, and the forces of darkness and emotion and body.

I am far from the only woman to grow up despising her own sex. Yet, when all is said and done, I was not a lawyer's son, I was a lawyer's daughter. The day would inevitably come when I would have to make a choice between a career, which is a man's destiny, or a woman's lot of marriage and motherhood. We weren't given a choice in those days. This was the fifties, and it was one or the other, not both. You can't have it all, girls. Choose.

By senior year, I was already accustomed to pulling my intellectual punches, to softening or masking my competitive drive.

Choose—

I thought I could postpone the evil moment. I applied to all-women's colleges, because it seemed to me that there I might be able to exercise an undivided mind and an undivided heart. In a women's college I could enjoy intellectual cut-and-thrust without fear of social unpopularity.

Smith and Wellesley were two of the Seven Sisters, women's colleges that, in prestige and scholarship, were the equivalent of the Ivy League Harvards and Yales, which then and for years to come barred women.

I visited Smith, I visited Wellesley, I liked them both, but the atmosphere at Smith seemed friendlier, so I decided that Smith was my first choice.

All prestigious colleges then sent out their acceptances and rejections simultaneously in one fateful spring week. Fat envelopes contained many forms to be filled out and returned. Thin envelopes said simply, No.

On the same day that fat envelopes arrived for me from Smith and Wellesley, my friends Irma and Dilla got their fat envelopes.

I'm going to Smith!

I'm going to Wellesley, said Irma.

Wellesley, said Dilla.

Come to Wellesley, said both.

Okay, I said.

And so, after such mature deliberation, I chose, and in September of 1952, with my friends, I entered Wellesley College as a member of the Class of '56, to major in economics and, who knows, perhaps some day, even go to law school—

But before I leave home for another unknown world, I want to take time out to remember another experience in yet another kind of world. It lasted only a day, and besides, nothing really happened. Nonetheless it was a magical day, a kind of coda to this chapter about what I learned in my high school years.

My father's legal secretary was a woman named MaryAnn, who thought the sun rose and set on him, and on my mother, and our whole family.

One day all of us were invited up to her parents' home in the country. MaryAnn's father, Joseph, had come from Czechoslovakia as a young man. He was a jeweler and a watchmaker, and could do anything with his skillful hands.

I had never seen a house surrounded by so many trees and fields and gardens and meadows and lawns. There were fruit trees, and currant bushes, and raspberries, and tomatoes and green peppers and corn, all growing in abundance. There were woods with trails that went on for miles, and little clearings with rustic swings or tables and chairs. Mr. Powley was tall and lean and reserved, while Mrs. Powley was little and redheaded and cantankerous, a peppery Irishwoman who only came up to her husband's chest, but who bossed him around anyway. She took us down to her "cellar," where glass jars of tomatoes and beans and jellies glowed ruby and emerald and gold. Her tall husband bragged about what a wonderful cook and housekeeper she was, and she twisted the corner of her apron and muttered fiercely at him to stop his teasing.

I've never seen another house quite like theirs. Mr. Powley had built it himself, with his jeweler's hands. He'd mixed concrete and poured it into foundations and walls that climbed up a hillside, following no blueprints, no plans, just the contours of the hill, all higgledy-piggledy. And inside the house, too, one room bore no particular logical relation to another, they just went up and down as they chose. You could wander comfortably up one step and down three, around a corner, then up or down again. There was a big dining-room table with a lace cloth on it in one room, yet instead, we ate outside, right by a brick fireplace (he'd made that, too) on which Mr. Powley cooked steaks for us. (Nobody barbecued, at least not in the East, in those days.) We ate corn that we had helped him to pick, and salad right from the garden, and bread Mrs. Powley had made, spread with some of her own jellies.

After dinner, our parents and the Powleys sat around and talked while MaryAnn, not far from girlhood herself, took my sister and me for a long hike along the trails through the woods. Then we stood in the wooden swing that Mr. Powley had made and swung back and forth, back and forth, as the sun began to dip toward the horizon.

It was dusk when we began rousing ourselves to leave. I went back alone into the house to go to the bathroom before the long trip home. It was silent and even more mysterious in the half-light and I got lost

finding the bathroom, and lost again finding my way back. But the
dusk was friendly, not scary. And I passed one room where a light was
glowing. Not an electric light, not a proper candle, but a rosy red
light, so I peeked in. No one was in there. But on a table in the empty
room stood a statue of a lady, wearing a cape with a hood, a big statue
it was, and in front of it, in front of her, a candle burned in a little red
cup, and that was the glowing red light.

How can I describe what I felt?

Awe, perhaps. I felt that I was invading some special kind of pri-
vacy, that I didn't belong there, that I shouldn't even look too closely
at the statue. And I also knew, in a way that wasn't thinking, but
knowing, that *this* was the heart of the house, this dim empty room in
which a red light glowed before a lady's statue.

I never mentioned the statue and the red light to anyone, never
asked what or who it was.

It was a mystery, and I guess I knew intuitively that the best thing to
do with a mystery was to leave it be. But I never forgot it, or the
Powleys, or MaryAnn, or the house and the light that burned in a dim
empty room at the heart of the house, at the heart of that day in the
country.

God Is Love?

ON MINISTRARI , SED MINISTRARE .

N Not to be ministered unto, but to minister. The motto of Wellesley College.

Which we, her daughters of the Class of 1956, translated in the time-honored tradition, Not to be ministers, but to be ministers' wives.

By the time I went off to Wellesley in September 1952, it was one of the most prestigious women's colleges in the country, one of the "Seven Sisters," a kind of female Ivy League. The most intellectual high school girls, tops in their class, then and for years to come, were barred from their natural habitats, Harvard, Yale, Princeton, and the like, which were strictly for men.

One of my first impressions of Wellesley was the diversity of the student body. Our class came from all parts of the country, even from abroad, in all sizes and shapes, although hardly all colors. There were numerous Oriental girls, because Mme. Chiang Kai-shek had gone to Wellesley, so there was a tradition; but there were no more than two black girls in our class. We had all kinds of last names, although only 10 percent of them belonged to Jewish girls, because there were strict quotas on the admission of Jews in those days.

Despite the diversity, we were from early on inculcated with a strong *esprit de corps.* We were all Wellesley women together. Very important. We were *women.*

Wellesley was then, as it still is, primarily a residential college. We new "adults" were therefore subject to strict parietal rules because it was understood, especially by our parents, who paid the bills, that Wellesley had adopted us as her daughters in the fullest sense and that she would stand *in loco parentis* to us while we were away, and guide us in social proprieties.

Accordingly, there were elaborate and rigid rules to regulate our dating. Rules were strictest for freshmen: our curfew was ten o'clock, with once a week permission for eleven-thirty, and a set number of one o'clocks for the semester. We had to sign in and out, listing our escort by name, our destination, our departure time, and our estimated time of reentry. If we were late coming back, we got "irregularities." Enough irregularities, and one lost going-out privileges. More than enough, or of a *certain kind,* added up to expulsion. And people *were* expelled. Not often, but it happened. Coming back drunk, for instance, would do it. Wellesley was a dry campus in a dry town. And anyway, we were *ladies.* Drunkenness was not tolerated. Neither, presumably, was fornication, but the evidence was easier to conceal. Drunkenness showed. Pregnancy, which also shows, was grounds for expulsion and, when we entered, so was marriage, but the rule about married students was relaxed after much strenuous debate by the time our class were juniors.

When I think about the whole elaborate setup, I marvel. Even the most rebellious of us never rose in protest, but instead bent and subverted the rules. That those rules were legitimate was assumed by us without question. I do think that it is peculiarly quaint, and very characteristic, that infractions should have been called "irregularities."

Wellesley's daughters would never bluntly call a spade a spade, let alone a bloody shovel.

We were *ladies*.

It was at Wellesley that this Brooklyn hoyden learned to be a lady. It took me a while, but by the time I graduated I could pour tea gracefully, speak WASP, put strangers at their ease, and hold my own in all sorts of social situations.

It's easy enough now to make fun of those long-ago morals and manners, and maybe a lot of it deserves to be made fun of.

And yet—

I have always been grateful for a polish which I would not have had otherwise, which enables me to feel comfortable with a great variety of people in a great variety of situations.

Above all I have been grateful to Wellesley for the sense of *entitlement* she gave me.

I am a Wellesley woman.

These days when bright girls go as a matter of course to Harvard and Yale and MIT, such a declaration is less impressive. But in my day, that statement was a password. It provided a resume, it was credentials.

I went to Wellesley.

It wasn't even necessary to say it to anyone. It was sufficient that *I* knew it. The sense of entitlement is a very powerful thing. Friends of mine have often been in a position where they have no money, but they have never been poor. What makes the difference? Entitlement.

Look at the defeated, at the women and the children congregating inside Manhattan's notorious welfare hotels, and you'll see what I mean.

I'm one of the lucky ones.

I am a Wellesley woman, and, by virtue of my education, entitled.

Despite the temptations of pleasurable courses in literature and French and art history, I stuck stubbornly to my original goal at Wellesley. Even though anything theoretical bored me to distraction, I became an economics major. Economics was a *serious* pursuit.

In any event, study is hardly the whole story of my four years at Wellesley.

I was also seriously involved with another strand of life, one that had preoccupied me since junior high, "looking for the boys."

And not me alone. There is an old joke: What kind of degree do you want to get? An M.R.S.! That joke was also reality for a lot of us at Wellesley. Maybe most of us. We were seeking academic excellence, it's true. But we were also husband hunting, and who's to say which quest took priority. After all, if you're going to spend your whole life with one man, and have to live your life through him, well, he'd better be the right one. And how do you know? How much rides on that one decision!

And so I was searching. Tall ones, short ones, lean ones, chubby ones, friendly ones, cruel ones, I was looking them all over. So many men, so little time. The ones who yearned for me, who wanted to marry me, I had no use for them. The ones I yearned for, wanted to marry, they strung me along on a fine-drawn string.

Some fun, some heartache.

Always a divided heart.

That was the real problem. I wasn't wholehearted about my education, any more than I was wholehearted about my goal in life. I was still torn by the same conflict I'd experienced in high school: ambition or popularity, career or marriage, the internal War Between Men and Women.

And so, internally sabotaged, I missed out on Phi Beta Kappa by a hair, was a Wellesley College Scholar instead of a Durant Scholar, scored tops on the Law Aptitude test but didn't apply to law school, because my forces were divided and frittered away. What do you want to be when you grow up? A man or a woman? What do you want to be when you grow up? A protagonist or an auxiliary?

The process that had begun in junior high intensified, the one that identified boys as doers and girls as hangers-on, followers. Most Wellesley women of my generation dropped out of the work force, if they ever entered it at all, to become wives, mothers, volunteer workers, unpaid pillars of society. Wellesley wasn't exactly a revolutionary mother, after all. How realistic is it to expect her to have been immune from the prevailing values of our time? We brought those values to college with us. Wellesley didn't overturn our goals: she taught us to achieve them, and to function exceedingly well in our allotted spheres.

So much for women's entitlement, even at Wellesley.

Then there was a third strand to my life at Wellesley, which was— Let's just call it Something Else. Something Apart. Or maybe, Being Jewish.

Great Neck was the first world I had entered that had Christians in it, a majority of Christians. Well, Wellesley College was an even more Christian world. The Jewish quota was 10 percent of the student body. No more, no matter how qualified. For the first time in my life, I was, and *felt,* part of a real minority.

Perhaps in reaction to such an overwhelmingly Christian environment, I made sure, at least on the holidays, to celebrate my Jewishness. When I could go home for Rosh Hashanah and Yom Kippur, I did so, although that wasn't often, because classes that were scheduled to be held on Jewish holidays were never canceled, as today they might well be. I could, and sometimes did, cut one day's classes, but I couldn't afford to cut two extra days for traveling to New York and back.

So when I couldn't go home for the holidays, I went in to Cambridge, to Hillel House, where observant Jewish students from the multitude of colleges and universities in the Boston area made up their own temporary family for worship. We had no identity crisis. We knew what was due to our God.

I did hear something about *their* God, though.

Wellesley's is an extraordinarily beautiful campus, sited on rolling, hilly ground, with lakes and ponds and groves and lawns; and graceful College Gothic spires and towers punctuate this lovely landscape.

One of these spires belongs to the Chapel, a nondenominational Christian chapel. Wellesley was ecumenical long before the word was common coin. But ecumenism doesn't mean interfaith. The Chapel had crosses in it.

I know, because Chapel attendance was obligatory on the first Sunday of the college year, when the sermon was always preached on the same text: God is Love.

That was carved in stone letters way high up under the beams: God is Love.

I was uncomfortable in the Chapel that first Sunday. Somewhat scandalized. So I didn't dare look too hard, or listen too closely.

But I heard that one all right.

God is Love?

For a moment, the thought was wonderful to me. And then I came to my senses.

If Christians believed *that,* they were softheaded and incredibly naive.

Maybe that's what made up Heaven, the Christian Heaven, out of fluff like that. Nice, all fluffy clouds and pink angel stuff, in a class with Santa Claus and the Easter Bunny.

I lived in the real world, thank you. And, I concluded, the Jewish world is a lot more real than the Christian world.

So I was very busy during my four years with books, dating, Judaism—

I was very busy at Wellesley.

But sometimes, walking to class across the meadow in the mist, or on a golden fall day, or sunbathing on the knob of the glacial hill next to our dorm, staring up into trees and sky, sometimes I stopped being busy, and just *was.*

I'd never before known the smiling face of Nature civilized and cherished by human heart and hand and mind. I didn't even know, all the four years I lived at Wellesley in that vast refreshing garden, that when I looked upon her face with longing and with love, that what I was seeing, in one of its aspects, was the natural face of God.

God is Love?

Traditional "step singing" at the college Chapel marked the beginning and end of the academic year. We sat on the steps by classes, and sang; and year after year, we shifted steps until at last it was my turn, I and my friends, to sit on the center steps, singing, singing, and then we rose and left as the song resounded behind us:

> *Where, oh, where have the seniors gone?*
> *Lost, lost in the wide, wide world.*

And then I too was gone from Wellesley, gone into the wide, wide world, leaving the Chapel, and its tantalizing inscription, behind me.

A Happy Ending

THIS IS HOW A MIRACLE HAPPENED.

In German, a miracle is a *Wunder.* A wonder. And this is a wonderful story I'm going to tell, a story full of wonders.

I was living in a fifth-floor walk-up in Brooklyn Heights with a roommate, Carol, a college friend with whom I had gone to Europe after graduation from Wellesley. Both of us were working in the brokerage firm that was then Merrill Lynch, Pierce, Fenner & Beane. I was editorial assistant on the employee magazine, *WE the People,* while Carol was a programmer in the infant computer department.

But, before I get on with it, I have to explain that, in order to be living in that apartment, I had undergone my father's curse.

"No decent woman lives in an apartment by herself. . . . She lives at home with her family. . . . Whores take apartments. . . . Why else does any woman want to live by herself? . . . To be a whore . . . If you move out, forget about ever coming back here. . . . If you move out, you're not my daughter anymore, you're a whore. . . ."

At the breakfast table, he said this, in front of my mother and sisters, who looked down at their plates. I was twenty-three years old.

But I did it anyway, my clothes and lots of books all packed up and picked up by a friend. I didn't even have to marry out of the faith to be disowned. All I had to do was leave home. That was enough.

Well, almost nothing is for eternity, and neither was my disowning, it turned out; although on that first morning it felt like a mortal blow, and, in fact, it wasn't healed—if that's what it is now, healed—until long past my father's death. My mother came to my apartment once, my father never, but after a few months I went back home for one Friday night, and nothing was said, so, given the custom of my family, the matter could be presumed to be settled. My father died without it ever being mentioned again: he never took back his curse, nor was he asked to, because I never told him what it had meant to me. Denial ruled our relationships, and "sorry" was a nonexistent concept for father and daughter alike. But I accepted the label my father gave me. It's important to remember that: I accepted the label. Retroactively, and for all time to come.

In fact, my romantic life in many ways had been a disaster area for a long time. It's still painful to recall, the pen is heavy in my hand.

The first serious relationship I'd had ran from my senior year in high school until the fall semester of my sophomore year at Wellesley. It suffered the usual teenage ups and downs, but had moved to "going steady," and John's timetable was set for pinning during sophomore year, engagement in junior year, marriage after graduation.

That panicked me.

I became claustrophobic: there were too many things to do, places to go, men to meet out there in the wide wide world for me to be confined so soon. My ambivalence was so profound I dared not recognize it for what it really was—an overwhelming fear of marriage. Most of my classmates and the culture at large saw marriage as the only possible successful conclusion of a woman's career goal. To me marriage represented something very different.

When I split with John, I thought I was just restless.

I began the dating game.

But ordinary dating, as long as it was with eligible Jewish men, was inextricably bound up with the larger issue of marriage. So, whenever I became "serious" about someone, old fears were reactivated, fears of the War Between Men and Women.

How can one be tender, loving, and respectful in wartime? How do I fraternize with the enemy?

Torn as I was by the twin pulls of desire and duty warring with dread of the loss of my freedom, I was unaware of the nature of this internal struggle. I was only miserable. I longed for the aloof men, spurned my suitors, I knew only unequal relationships.

Until I was twenty-two I remained a virgin: more common in those days, perhaps, than now. I offered up my virginity as a sacrifice to become *grown-up,* something I was not and thought everyone else was. To become *a real woman.* Like most sacrifices, it was in vain.

Having given the gift, of course, I had to love the recipient, and I did. Madly, passionately, in thrall. I was witty, charming, accommodating, all to please him. No Scheherazade was more anxious to captivate her sultan than I was to please and hold him, whom I placed at the center of my existence, displacing myself.

I had thought that the relationship was about *love.*

But it, like another long-term relationship of those years, was really about power. Not physical power struggles. About control, about submission, about domination.

And like most women of our culture, my role was the masochistic one.

Today there is an expanded vocabulary to describe my state. Dependency is a recognized syndrome, and abuse can be other than physical.

Then I just felt like I was crazy. Out of control. Desperate. Ashamed. And guilty. Always guilty.

Some of the guilt was from the teachings of the fathers: sex is bad, sex is wrong, sex is immoral. Some of it was the real thing, coming from deep within me, from what I could never then have understood as my *true self,* that part of me which knew intuitively that these relationships were unhealthy.

They did not nourish me, they ate away at my self-esteem, my psyche, my spirit. I was, not unexpectedly, frigid and anorgasmic.

Without recognizing it at all, I was sinking deeper and deeper into the condition of despair. I kept seeking love and reassurance in touching and holding, and all I found was exploitive sexuality.

That war between those natural enemies, men and women, was raging furiously, and there was no winning this war for me. Not in submission. Not in domination.

Where was that elusive man who would win the battle, settle the war, complete and validate my incomplete and insufficient self?

Some day my Prince will come.

The theme song of dependent women, women who love others too much and themselves too little.

What would eventually have become of me? I don't know.

Because at that point of peril and despair, along came Frank.

And now I can go back to the story, to the Once Upon a Time of Frank and me.

My father sublet office space to a young lawyer who was enough older than I to take an avuncular interest in my unmarried state. He said to my father, Judy doesn't have much opportunity to meet eligible Jewish men where she is. Now the group I belong to, the Henry Street Settlement, has lots of suitable people. The editor of our newsletter has done the job for two years now, and he doesn't want to do it anymore. Judy would be perfect as editor, she does it professionally already, and she'd help the group and meet nice people all at the same time. Should I call her?

My father asked my mother, who asked me.

My professional skills were requested? Prompted mostly by vanity, I said, Sure.

So the young lawyer called and told me about the group, which was not, as you may have thought, mini-social workers among the poor. Soup kitchens had gone out with the Great Depression, and who would ever have believed they'd be back in our midst fifty years later?

No, the Junior Group of the Henry Street Settlement was a social organization of solid middle-class Jewish young men and women of Manhattan, educated and eligible. The regular meetings acted as high-class, post-college mixers. There'd be talks, or skits, or we'd plan activities, parties and dances to raise funds for the Lower East Side settlement house, which was the reason for the Junior Group's existence. A fair amount of money *was* raised, and a fair number of suitable matches were also arranged.

It sounded okay to me. I would be able to meet all these other young people not as a peer, which would have terrified me into awkward and sullen shyness, but as an *editor*. But when the president of the group called with a formal offer of the volunteer position, he said that, because I was a newcomer, the retiring editor would stay on as titular coeditor and fill me in on the group and its activities.

I pondered that.

I didn't mind sharing the title. That was no problem. But, I said firmly, it would have to be quite clear that I was actually the editor, that editorial decisions would be mine. The president said I had better clear that with the person involved, the retiring editor himself.

He's very nice, said the president. His name is Frank Bruder.

So, all Wellesley snippiness, riding my highest horse, I called this Frank Bruder.

As long as it's understood that the editorial decisions are *mine,* I said grandly.

First wonder, he didn't hang up on me.

As long as you're ready to do all the work, he said, I don't care *what* you do, I didn't even want my name on the masthead any more, but they talked me into it.

So we agreed on the sharing of titles and the division of labor, and it never even occurred to me that I had been obnoxious. I was oblivious to all my usual baggage, the necessity to be feminine, to please the Jewish male ego, to cajole and flatter and charm; all the garbage had taken wing, flown out the window on the wings of my own pride and vanity.

What a liberation!

After all, who was this Frank Bruder anyway? I was under no romantic illusions about him. Who was he to me? A potential rival and obstacle, that's all. I didn't have to think about marrying *him,* thank heaven! I owed him nothing, I expected nothing, I was free to pursue my own way, my own ideas, my own plans. There *was* no war.

And so we set up our first meeting with prospective members of the newsletter committee on a weekday evening in September after work, in a deserted office on Fifty-seventh Street, and I arrived a little early to take the measure of this person with whom I would, willy-nilly, be yoked for a year.

He turned out to be—*nice.*

Pleasant.

Even attractive.

I wonder how grudging I was in that assessment. I was certainly very touchy about my authority and my autonomy. *I* would run the meeting, *I* would do this and that. *I* would even make the coffee. (This was before Women's Liberation; I saw making the coffee, not as a burden, but as part of the power.)

Don't use those cups, Frank warned. The hot coffee will melt the wax.

I didn't even bother to reply. I just made the coffee and poured a cup, and the wax melted, and it was undrinkable. So we found different cups.

I'll bet he said, I told you so, but he claims he didn't.

We also had a dispute about how many tablespoons of coffee to use in the pot. I won.

We served coffee right away to all the volunteers who'd shown up. Frank took one sip, made a face, then handed the cup back to me and said, When I want shoe polish, Judy, I'll ask for it.

Well.

We certainly started off even, didn't we.

When I tasted the coffee, though, I had to laugh. He was right. To this day, if you come to our house, you can be reassured that it will be Frank who makes the coffee. Unless you want shoe polish, in which case you can ask me for it.

Besides newsletter meetings, there were other committee meetings, and skits and activities of various kinds, and Frank and I got along fine.

He was really easy to be with. We worked together like friends.

I spoke as I pleased to him, said what I thought, didn't worry about effect, wasn't self-conscious.

We were comfortable together.

It was several months before he asked me for a date.

Frank lived in Manhattan, and I lived in Brooklyn Heights, so we decided (very avant garde, that was) to meet at the Metropolitan Museum, in front of the enormous painting of Rosa Bonheur's *Horse Fair*.

I arrived at the museum early that day (another little wonder, since at that time I was invariably late for everything), and as I stood on the corner, watching the crowd, suddenly I glimpsed an attractive man in a felt snap-brim hat. He was already a few feet past me when I realized that it was Frank. I called, and ran after him, and he turned, and came toward me, and we entered the museum arm in arm, laughing at the coincidence.

We decided to go and pay our respects to *Horse Fair* anyway, but when we arrived at the gallery of nineteenth-century paintings, we found—nothing.

No *Horse Fair*. Eight feet of painting, not there. Nowhere. The galleries were so jammed that we marveled at the luck of meeting by accident outside. It seemed a good omen.

But the next thing that happened was that he didn't ask me out for New Year's Eve.

Another wonder: I, emotional dependent and handmaiden, decided that I wasn't going to sit around and mope about Frank. I was going to have a good time by myself. I signed up for a tour of Puerto Rico. I had a fine, if unromantic, time, and came back refreshed and exhilarated, to a ringing telephone and several dates with Frank, the most important of which turned out to be a bitterly cold February night on the West Side Highway after the movies when the rear right tire suddenly went flat.

Frank got out and began to change the tire. He was having trouble, so I got out, too, and offered to help. He looked at me a little strangely, but I had never had any hesitation with Frank. I took the wrench and fitted it snugly over the first lug, stepped down hard in my high-heeled pump on the wrench, the nut loosened, and I unscrewed it.

I removed the nuts, loosened the tire, lifted it off, and asked him to lift the spare onto the rim. I could do it, I explained, but it was a little heavy, so—

He was stunned, he says.

Well, at Great Neck High School, where I'd taken Driver Education, you didn't pass the course unless you could change a tire in ten minutes. *Anybody.*

That, he told me later, was the moment he knew he was going to marry me.

There you were, a nice Jewish girl, all dressed up, in high heels, and you change a tire.

What did you expect me to do? I asked him. Leave you to freeze and do it alone?

Exactly, he said.

The course of true love gathered momentum.

There was the evening he said he would call me. But I was on the telephone from eight until ten, when the doorbell rang, and there was Frank, leaning against the wall, panting.

Call Mount Sinai Hospital, he said.

(That was his standard remark when he finally made it up the last of the five flights to our apartment.)

What are you doing here, I asked him, astonished. We didn't have a date or anything.

I was supposed to call you at nine, he said, and the line was busy, and busy, and busy, so I came over instead.

Finally Frank told me that the drives to Brooklyn and the five-flight climbs were ruining his health, that clearly it would be better for us to get married and live at a sensible altitude, and why didn't I move back home in the meantime.

So I did. And we were engaged, and had a huge garden party at my parents' home, with enormous quantities of food prepared by my mother. The high point of the afternoon was Frank's Great-aunt Dora's recitation of the poem she'd written to commemorate our engagement. Great-aunt Dora was about as big as a minute, and she carried a huge black lizard handbag. Before anyone realized, she'd conned the accordion player into turning the mike over to her, she'd whipped a poem out of her handbag, and begun.

O friendly motley crowd!

It went on interminably, but I stopped listening right after that first felicitous line, so simple, so perfect.

That line became one of those family catchphrases. It still is.

Catchphrases, stories, myths.

What I've been telling you is our family history, those stories that children want to hear again and again, How Daddy Met Mommy.

And here comes the happy ending.

The handsome Prince finally came. He was even a Jewish prince!

And there was a royal wedding, complete with three rabbis.

I said it was a miracle, didn't I? A miracle that at our first meeting I had been on my worst behavior, a miracle that Frank never bothered about that, a miracle that the result—surprise! surprise!—was freedom for me at last to be who I really was with a man, myself, not some cartoon, follow-the-dots figure of a nice, pleasing, marriageable Jewish girl. I never had to play dating games with Frank, let alone war games. A miracle.

And so we lived happily ever after.

A happy ending. Sort of.

For this is real life, not a fairy tale, and happy endings are partial. Complex. They have limited warranties and lots of fine print.

Remember, I had grown up cannon fodder in a War Between Men and Women since childhood, had been instructed in the doctrine of woman's bodily menace and the barter value of her flesh in the marital economy, and, for wishing to move out on my own, had been called a whore by my father.

It all stuck, all of it.

I was a good student. I learned these lessons about my sexuality long before I met my husband. Such lessons could not easily be unlearned just because three men in black robes intoned prayers and formulae over me.

When it came to marriage, you see, I turned away from sin, which at that time I understood as, well, perhaps not sexual intercourse entirely—after all, that was sanctioned in marriage, wasn't it?—but certainly the sin of sexual pleasure. Taking pleasure, feeling pleasure, is for whores. Not for respectable Jewish wives.

There were important lessons I had *never* learned. I didn't know that sexuality was not a separate compartment of me, that sexuality instead is the very root and heartspring of the self, that it is where creativity, spontaneity, and joy make their dwelling place.

I didn't know that I had an unhealed wound that still festered, didn't know that I was crippled, that in my very identity as a woman I was damaged goods. That knowledge was locked away, drowned in fathoms of unconsciousness; and so I turned with my whole heart to this relationship that promised hope and a new life.

I had come through, I had arrived in traditional safe harbor, I had fulfilled my destiny.

I was a Jewish bride.

Ordinary Time

OST OF THE CHURCH YEAR is lived in what is called ordinary time, a time of everyday living, as distinguished from the great seasons of anticipation and celebration marked out in their own liturgical colors on the church calendar, the hopeful waiting of Advent and the grateful radiance of Christmas, soul-exploring Lenten penance and the resurrection joy of Eastertide.

Purple for penance, white for joy. But ordinary time is green, the color of things that grow out of the earth, not celestial, but earthbound, not the stuff of dreams, but things that are real and tangible.

And ordinary.

Commonplace, even. Like grass. Or the leaves on trees.

I was grateful that my marriage had brought me into ordinary time.

We were a newly married couple like thousands of others, commonplace, ordinary, but our lives were special to us.

The *lune de miel,* honeymoon, is a special time, a happy time. We loved each other, we loved our tiny one-room apartment in Brooklyn Heights. Frank loved his new job; he, too, was now working at Merrill

Lynch, as a broker-trainee. We were playing house. Until, after a year and a half, we started thinking about children. Oh, not right now, this very minute. But sometime in the not-too-distant future. Folk wisdom said conception took around six months of trying. Well, we might as well get ready for that future. Before our lease was up, we had moved to an apartment with a bedroom, out in Great Neck.

It's greener there, more parks, better for children, we reasoned.

Money would be tight; but we were young enough, hopeful for the future, and in love: what more is needed in the beginning? We would just be even more careful about budgeting; and so we developed a simple system, the Bruder Envelope System of banking. We labeled a bunch of plain white letter-size envelopes with outgoing categories. Every payday we stuffed each envelope with its appropriate cash amount, and kept them all in a shoebox in the closet until the monthly bill paying. Every month brought its own crisis, which we solved by literally shuffling dollars, robbing one envelope to pay another, a personal, hands-on system of financial planning. It worked well enough.

We also tackled family planning.

That too was simple.

I stopped using a diaphragm.

But nothing happened.

Folk wisdom's six months sped by, and every month I cramped, and bled, and nothing happened. More months. Still nothing happened. It's early yet, people reassured us. Maybe it's physical and mental stress, you know, working and commuting full-time. Maybe if you stayed home, relaxed, enjoyed yourself—

We stopped and took a look at our lives.

Frank was optimistic about his future at Merrill Lynch. I was restless, though. My title was grander than before and my salary higher, but I was still doing essentially the same job on the employee magazine I had started with five years ago. And I didn't want another job. I wanted a baby. So I "retired" from Merrill Lynch to become a full-time housewife. I would follow that good advice—I would stay home, relax, and enjoy myself.

And I did.

We joined the Conservative temple where we had been married. This was not exactly a spiritual act. God for me had dwindled to china services (six sets, one everyday meat, one everyday milk, one "company" meat and one "company" milk, all for ordinary time, as it were, and one meat and one milk for the special celebration of Passover) and silverware (six sets, ditto all around, not all of silver, naturally, most were stainless steel). God was also a convenient kosher butcher, which we hadn't had in Brooklyn Heights. And God was the many hours we logged in temple with my parents celebrating two days of Rosh Hashanah, the entire fast day of Yom Kippur, the long mornings of other, lesser holidays. God meant two identical seders, back to back, the entire Haggadah recited in Hebrew from beginning to end each time, the same songs, same cast of characters, instant replay. All of this for Frank, who was not brought up to it, didn't understand it, didn't enjoy it, was boring and unrewarding, but he was uncomplaining, because it meant so much to me.

And what did it mean to me?

That if we did all those things, used enough different dishes, put in enough hours at services, why, then, nothing terrible would happen, and we would live happily, and Jewishly, ever after.

We made friends through the temple. I lunched, I shopped, I read, I volunteered.

There was still too much time, and I set about filling up the voids.

I wrote play and restaurant reviews for a hotel magazine in exchange for second-night theater tickets and a strange medley of meals, and assured myself that Grub Street journalism kept my hand in, and my mind from vegetating.

That was very important to me, to be able to hang on to an image of myself as a writer, student, thinker. Not *merely* a housewife.

When the United Nations Association's Great Neck chapter asked me to edit their monthly newsletter, I agreed.

But there was still time left over.

To fill the chinks, I turned to my old reliable standby.

I read.

I was as compulsive about reading as any alcoholic about booze, gambler about horses, nymphomaniac about men. I used reading for the same purposes all compulsives use their compulsions, distraction, compensation, consolation, escape, to keep the goblins of fear and anxiety at bay. When the formless yearning which I didn't even recognize as loneliness and emptiness flooded over me, I opened a book.

So time passed pleasantly enough, years of it.

The only terrible thing that happened was—

Nothing happened.

My sister Mindy, who had married six months after me, became pregnant.

How happy everyone was!

I even envied her morning sickness, her growing shapelessness, all of it.

What about *you?* people would say, and smile.

Frank and I were godparents for my nephew Larry. I was happy to be a godparent. But the envy was there, always gnawing.

Mentchen bei dir! exclaimed people at the *brith,* the party celebrating Larry's circumcision. The same to you!

Alevai! I breathed to myself. From your mouth into God's ear.

But nothing happened.

We got a dog. Unlike babies, dogs could be had for the asking, or for the buying. I poured out all my unfulfilled desires onto our Hungarian sheep dog's shaggy being. We took him wherever we went, with his little "Beekman kit," a flight bag packed with brushes and grooming tools and a training leash, a parody of a diaper bag!

But even Beekman couldn't fill an empty womb forever.

It was time to *do* something, I said to the gynecologist.

We did what could be done over twenty years ago, which wasn't very much. X rays, temperature taking, boosting Frank's sperm, artificial insemination—a calculated, messy procedure whose details I spare you because my memory of it has mercifully blurred over the years. All of it, thermometers, charts, test strips, rubber caps, were about as far removed from any spontaneous joy in lovemaking as one can imagine. And anyway, nothing worked.

Something that ordinary people have happen to them almost by accident, often against their will and desire, was beyond our control.

There is an old joke about an American woman who goes to a famous French doctor because she wants a baby and can't seem to have one. The doctor tries every procedure possible on her, but at last he calls the husband into his consulting room. Alas, Monsieur, he says, your wife, she is impregnable. That is, your wife, she is inconceivable. No, no, that is not it. Your wife, she is *unbearable*.

That's it.

I was unbearable.

The superachiever was a failure, a failure as a woman.

Again my sister became pregnant.

How about you? people would say, still smiling, but more pointedly.

What's the matter, don't you like children? they accused.

The emptiness!

The empty womb.

My sister's second son was born.

Frank and I began to talk about adoption.

A cousin, a doctor in California, magically intervened. And so I had my first baby in the beauty parlor, three thousand miles from the delivery room, while fellow customers and operators applauded as I took the long-distance telephone call.

It's a girl!

A beautiful, healthy baby girl.

We were on a plane to California the next morning.

Take your little girl and go quickly, said the doctors.

Cradling that tiny being to myself, feeling the miniature fingers curl around mine, caressing the satin skin, I was euphoric. My bubble was painfully pricked by my cousin's son's spontaneous remark at the dinner table the night before we left for New York. Well, what about her mother? he said. *She's* not happy tonight.

Our happiness, then, came with a price tag, another woman's sorrow.

Most adoptive parents have a hidden anxiety, certainly in the beginning: am I worthy? Natural parents simply *have* their children. Adoptive parents somehow have to earn them. Today, tomorrow, every day, earn them anew, not *our* children really. Ours on suffrance.

The only time we ever flew first class was the day we brought Jane Elizabeth home in a basket between us from California to New York. (Would she have had a happier life in the California sunshine? I thought suddenly.)

Jane Elizabeth.

Henna Elisheva.

Jane, for Jane Austen, and Elizabeth for Elizabeth Bennet, the forthright heroine of Jane Austen's *Pride and Prejudice*. Henna, for Hannah, her maternal great-grandmother, and Henna for grace, because *hen* (pronounced with a gutteral *ch* at the beginning) is the Hebrew word for grace and loving-kindness. Elisheva is just the Hebrew translation of Elizabeth.

My womb was still empty, but now my arms were filled, and my life, and my emptiness. I had a daughter, my second chance, my daughter, my self.

All the mistakes, the angers, the resentments, the needs, the desires, everything wounded in my life, I could make up for now. My daughter would have everything I ever wanted. My daughter would *never* be unhappy like I was.

That was true enough.

My daughter has never been unhappy like I was. She has been unhappy in her own way, the unhappiness that inevitably results from being an object of someone else's regards and needs, rather than a subject in one's own right. But who knows such things in advance?

Jane was a beautiful baby, so beautiful that I grew accustomed to strangers stopping me in the street to admire her. I loved that. I had always felt ugly, always, what seemed like my whole life I had felt ugly, and Jane's beauty somehow transformed my ugliness. All unaware, I was taking possession of her beauty.

Oh, we were happy!

Frank was in love with his girl-child. He gave her bottles, and sang to her, "The Cannibal King with the Big Nose Ring," and "I Went to the Animal Fair," and he made up games for her and played with her. I wasn't a very good player, but I could hold her when she was sick, and rock with her in the rocking chair, and sing "Aye Lye Lu Lu Babeleh" to her.

All was well with us.

At last my emptiness was filled.

I spent my days in the park across the street, joined the other mothers and babies on the park benches, talked formula and diapers and recipes and husbands' foibles. At last I had been accepted into the sisterhood of women. I belonged.

Even during the long dying of Frank's father and, then, within twelve months, his mother's drastic deterioration from chronic asthma and her death, even in all this emotional darkness, Jane was our light, our comfort, the new life of her, the promise, a bubble of happiness that kept us afloat.

After the deaths, life leveled out again. We were living in ordinary time. Wonderful, blessed ordinary time.

I had everything I wanted.

And yet—

There was still a restlessness somewhere within. The ambivalence, still. Domestic world? Wider world?

The mothers on the park benches, the cozy conversations, the gossip, the complacency, it was—

It was boring.

I didn't realize I was bored. Actually I concluded, I don't belong after all. I thought I did, but I don't. They're all content, those other happy women. There must be something wrong with me. My fault.

And then I met Sally.

It didn't take long to recognize that we were two of a kind, two misfits in the park.

Sally was Gentile—a small-town, upstate New York, WASP-type Gentile. With a master's degree in sociology, and not socially poised

and self-confident like our sister park-sitters, but soft-spoken, diffi-
dent, almost shy. She didn't even wear makeup! And her little girl,
among all the Melissas and Amys and Stephanies, was named, of all
things, Kendal. It was a family name.

Like I said, different.

I wasn't obviously different like Sally. I didn't look or sound or act
very different from anybody else. But I was. And somehow, by mag-
netism, or vibration, however that works, Sally and I recognized one
another.

Kindred spirits.

Away from the park benches, down by the sandbox, while Jane and
Kendal spilled sand in and out of pails and on each other, or at the
baby swings, while we pushed, we talked and talked, about books,
about France, about ideas, about books some more. We wheeled our
daughters' strollers up and down Middle Neck Road, and we talked.

We talked about wanting to read James Joyce's monumental epic,
Ulysses, but neither of us having the nerve to try it by ourselves.

And we made a decision. We would buy Stuart Gilbert's guide to
Ulysses, and we would embark on our own odyssey, reading it chapter
by chapter, with commentary, then wrestling with it.

Which we did.

One single day in the life of Leopold Bloom, a childless Irish Jew in
Dublin in 1904 searching for a son he never had, that's all *Ulysses* is
about, but it took us months to work our way from the opening scene,
a mock Mass, all the way to the rapturous climax of Molly Bloom's
forty-four-page single-sentence soliloquy:

> yes and then he asked me would I yes to say yes my mountain flower
> and first I put my arms around him yes and drew him down to me so he
> could feel my breasts all perfume yes and his heart was going like mad
> and yes I said yes I will Yes.

And Bloom led his "son" Stephen home, and Molly said yes, and
regretfully, lovingly, Sally and I finished *Ulysses,* and Jane and Kendal

learned to walk and slide down the sliding pond, and we said yes we said yes we would go back to school, each of us, yes, Sally, who had her M.A., to study for a doctorate, and I, to begin a master's degree in English literature, yes, we would, yes.

And furthermore, just as Bloom had "adopted" Stephen, so Frank and I had applied to the Louise Wise Adoption Service, and shortly after I had finished my epic journey with Sally, Frank and I were offered a son, and we said yes to John Simon, and yes to a house in Roslyn, and that simple decision, to read a book, had far-reaching consequences, and all of them were Yes.

Per Una Selva Oscura

HAT SEMESTER HOFSTRA UNIVERSITY was offering a seminar on James Joyce, which seemed providential; and so, at the age of thirty-three, I became a student again.

My confidence about my academic ability lasted about fifteen minutes into the first session of the first seminar. What were these people talking about? I felt, probably for the first time in my entire academic life, that I was out of my league, that I was overwhelmed.

For several weeks I was in despair, tempted to back out and return to the park and the swings and the stove and the diapers where I obviously belonged. Only the fact that I loved the reading, that James Joyce himself, far from being incomprehensible, spoke through his works directly to my heart, kept me in the class.

One evening I talked to the professor about my problem with class discussions. He assured me that I was simply being dazzled by fancy footwork, by a graduate school vocabulary and jargon and methods of focusing of which I was ignorant. I began to listen harder, and it wasn't long before I realized he was right. I even developed the capacity to bullshit in this new language. But I found myself increasingly reluctant to exercise that capacity, which had never troubled me before in my undergraduate years. Something had changed.

Joyce mattered too much to me to bullshit about.

He was too important.

Literature was too important.

We read *The Dubliners* in that seminar, Joyce's only collection of short stories, unlike any others with which I was familiar, less concerned with plot or psychology than with the *quidditas* of things, as Thomas Aquinas calls it, their *that-ness,* their truth, the essential self or being. Epiphanies, that's what Joyce's stories were, from the Greek word meaning *showing,* the moment, a quasi-divine moment, in which the essence of something or someone shows forth. His Dubliners are shown, not changing or developing, but simply as they are.

Epiphanies.

I did a final paper, got an A for the seminar, and was hooked. I loved my husband in my heart, my two children in my gut, but in a classroom my head came alive.

Next I took a course in Shakespeare and after that a course on the seventeenth-century metaphysical poet John Donne, who stimulated and provoked my imagination just as Joyce had.

He was a courtier, a playboy, a poet, a husband, a clergyman, a dark, handsome brooding man whose desires ran in many, and conflicting, directions, and whose soul in consequence was torn.

His love poetry treats the subject as if it were sacred; while his religious poetry treats his relationship with God in explicitly erotic, often directly sexual terms.

He wrote what I think are the sexiest lines in English poetry, addressed to his mistress:

> License my roving hands, and let them go
> Before, behind, between, above, below.
> O my America! my new-found-land . . .

And also this amazing sonnet, addressed to God:

Batter my heart, three-personed God; for You
As yet but knock, breathe, shine, and seek to mend;
That I may rise, and stand, o'erthrow me, and bend
Your force, to break, blow, burn and make me new.
I, like an usurped town, to another due,
Labor to admit you, but Oh, to no end!
Reason, your viceroy in me, me should defend,
But is captived, and proves weak or untrue.
Yet dearly I love You, and would be loved fain,
But am betrothed unto Your enemy.
Divorce me, untie, or break that knot again,
Take me to You, imprison me, for I
Except You enthrall me, never shall be free,
Nor ever chaste, except You ravish me.

Nor ever chaste, except You ravish me.

What an image: God as ravisher, brutal lover, rapist—whom we, who yearn for Love, beg to bring us to our knees, flat on our backs, vanquished, to receive it. Or Him.

The man who wrote that sonnet knew in his very gut that God and Love and Sex are all entangled, are involved with one another in a single drama, not separate elements, parts sacred, parts profane, parts corporeal, parts spiritual, but all of a piece, one flesh, one body and soul and spirit intermingled. For me, then, John Donne, like James Joyce, tells it like it is: jealousy, morbidity, drama, grotesquerie and all, this is it, he says, this is the way it is for us human creatures.

I got A's in all three graduate courses; I could now matriculate at Hofstra as a candidate for a master's degree in English literature. But the rest of Hofstra's program followed a fixed curriculum, offered only during the daytime. Being a student now was more complicated for me. I was Frank's wife also, and I was a mother. There were the normal demands of mothering, birthday parties, teacher-parent conferences, unexpected viruses, there was shopping and cooking and cleaning, all the routine of life colliding with my need (and my desire) to study, to prepare papers, to sit quietly and think. Many women cope with the various demands of wearing several hats. What made it difficult for me (as it may for lots of others also) was my internal split. Whichever I was doing, studying or mothering, I felt guilty because I wasn't doing the other. I was torn by guilt and by desire. A harried young woman friend recently asked me for some wisdom on child-rearing.

Hah! My wisdom on child-rearing—

But one thing came up from deep within. If I had it to do again, I said, I would do *whatever* I was doing with a single heart. I would do one thing at a time, I said. That is what Zen practice calls one-pointedness; and I believe it is one meaning of the beatitude, Blessed are the pure in heart.

One thing at a time. That's the key.

How I wish I had possessed that key at the time. But no matter how guilty I felt at neglecting my children "in my heart," having tasted the sweetness of a pursuit that belonged to the essential me, I wasn't about to give it up.

If I could only find a master's program that was more flexible in its requirements than Hofstra's, that offered classes in the evening, it would keep practical difficulties to a minimum. Frank always encour-aged me to do what would help me grow as *me*. He was more reliable than any baby-sitter, and he was unfailingly supportive and enthusiastic and encouraging.

Having sought, I found; and in 1969 I enrolled as a master's degree candidate at nearby C. W. Post College. I planned to take one, at most two, classes a semester. I wasn't in any hurry, I was studying for myself; I projected no future from my studies.

School was the lifeline to my self. That's all.

At C. W. Post I studied modern poetry, seventeenth- and eigh-teenth-century poetry and prose, the history of the English language, Shakespeare again, Chaucer and Middle English literature. I had two extraordinary professors, Richard Griffith, who taught medieval litera-ture and culture, and Jeanne Welcher Kleinfield, whose special field at Post was the eighteenth century. As a bonus, Grif and Jeanne became our friends. I mention these friendships because, in a curious way, they alleviated a little of my feeling selfish at using time and money just for me. That my teachers became *our* friends meant that I brought my studies home, as it were, to become transmuted into something for both of us, for Frank as well as for me.

My life was thoroughly busy now. I was juggling all its elements with more ease and skill, and I had little time left over for niggling doubts and questions, for anxieties and unease. It was a productive time, a happy time.

And then it was over.

In June 1973, in cap and gown, under threatening skies, with my husband and children and parents watching, I rose to receive my M.A. in English literature. The ceremony beat out a deluge by moments, and then it was a laughing race pell-mell across the field to shelter, and there I was, an M.A., my occupation gone.

Once again, the question stared me in the face: what are you going to be when you grow up, little girl?

That's where I was in the summer of 1973. Still not knowing.

I could rest on this recent laurel, devote full time to housewifery and motherhood, like— Well, like a *normal* woman is supposed to, and be content with that.

That had somehow never been enough. Why should it be so now?

I could go on to get a Ph.D. in literature. Getting a master's degree had been fun. I had done it at my own pace, for no purpose but my own delight. But a Ph.D.! That's serious stuff, that's for grown-ups, that implies a serious goal. A Ph.D. is a *professional* degree. Can I be a professional? Can a woman be a wife, a mother, and also a scholar?

Who will give me permission?

Where do I go for guidance?

I wanted to make up my own mind. In college I had majored in economics because everyone expected me to major in English. Following other people's advice and acting directly contrary to it each amount, in the end, to the same thing: submission and dependency.

As for God, well, whatever he had been in my life, he had never been counsel or oracle. Whatever prayer was for me, it wasn't asking God for guidance. And what was God for me these days, anyway?

God, as I conceived him, had become more transcendent than ever, had retreated farther into the deepest heavens. I wouldn't think of praying to one so far away for guidance. I wouldn't dream of it.

And yet, when at last I received the sign for which I was waiting, that was exactly the form in which it came—a dream. But not just an ordinary dream, of course. It was what the psychologist Carl Gustav Jung called a "big" dream. As people enter upon midlife, the great passage from the first, active half of their life to the second, reflective half is heralded by a dream.

I had not thought of my dilemma as a midlife crisis. It was just a decision that for some reason I couldn't seem to make one way or the other. There was no doubt, however, that I was squarely in midlife. In November 1973 I celebrated my thirty-ninth birthday, and entered my fortieth year of life.

Forty is a powerful number.

After the Exodus, the Israelites wandered in the desert for forty years until they had been transformed into a free people able to take possession of a new land. Moses fasted on the mountain for forty days and forty nights before he received the tablets of the Ten Commandments from the hand of God. Long before that, rain fell for forty days and forty nights to flood the world. And long afterward, Jesus fasted in the desert for forty days and forty nights, assailed by demon temptations, to purify himself for his coming mission.

Women, especially, have tended to see forty as the end of life rather than its beginning, and to deny their own coming-of-age. Because it is also a coming-of-age, make no doubt about that.

There are all kinds of dreams, funny, absurd, boring, menacing. What Jung referred to as a big dream is one which is associated with a major event in one's life, and has an unmistakable haunting, symbolic, and prophetic quality that makes it almost *numinous,* charged with the force and radiance generally associated with the divine. Jung wrote a great deal about archetypes, which are eternal patterns of power, undying realities, such images as The Father, The Mother, The Bride,

The Trickster. Often a big dream marks the coming of an archetype, to transmit information or knowledge or advice, to bring a message from The Self (the universal essence in which we all participate, and which is within us) to the unique particular self which is you or me.

Perhaps it wasn't surprising, then, that the sign which came to me at this point of decision was a dream. I had been living for months with the question of what to do with my life, whether to go on with academic studies or return to being a full-time wife, mother, home-maker.

This, then, was the dream.

I was at a party, a big noisy crowded party, in the Manhattan apartment of a friend of ours. Frank and Jane and John were also at the party, but there were so many people that I wasn't actually with them, we were all scattered among the crowd. I wandered into the bedroom, and then into the adjoining bathroom, but when I came out, I wasn't back in the bedroom again. I had come back out the same door I had entered, but I had come out into somewhere else. I was in a dark, echoing room, an enormous room that at first seemed to be empty. As my eyes grew accustomed to the dimness, I saw that it wasn't empty, that scattered here and there on the bare wood floor were tables and chairs, all made of bare unadorned wood. There was no one else there, only me, and the vast dark room, and the wooden forms of furniture, and suddenly there were words, emblazoned on my mind and echoing there so that I "saw" them and "heard" them without actually doing either.

In a dark wood—

I was in a dark wood, strayed and lost in a dark wood.

Even in the dream, I recognized where those words came from, I "heard" it in Italian and in English:

> *Nel mezzo del cammin di nostra vita*
> *Mi ritrovai per una selva oscura . . .*

In English I could remember three lines, not just two; and they are the opening lines of Dante's *Divine Comedy:*

> Halfway along the journey of our life,
> Having strayed from the right path and lost it,
> I awoke to find myself in a dark wood.

This is the opening stanza of the "Inferno," Dante's descent into Hell, into the realm of the damned souls. As I heard those words in the dream, I recognized their truth for me, that I had strayed from the straight path, and was lost.

I understood very well what it meant for me to be standing there, lost, in that cavernous dim room. But how could I find the path back to the party, to friends and family, back to the place I had come from? Then I noticed on the opposite wall, faint in the dimness, two doors and a button panel: an elevator. Now I had a choice. I could try and find my way back through this dark wood, try and retrace my steps, or I could take the elevator down to the ground floor, then back up to find the party all over again, from the bottom up.

I stood there in the silence, alone, at a crossroads, trying to decide which way to go, not knowing, still profoundly undecided. As I stood there, I heard a faint rustling sound coming toward me from the far reaches of the room, a rustling, as of taffeta, perhaps. And then there began to emerge from the deep shadows a band of women. Even before I could see them, I knew that they were beautiful, graceful blond women wearing gowns of palest blue, and they came toward me swiftly. But they didn't speak to me, because I suddenly knew that their leader was coming, the leader of that band of women, and she would tell me what to do, which direction to take. And so I waited for her, this woman in blue, because she was about to appear, she was near at hand, and then I would know, and then—

I woke up.

It was all vanished, the dark room with its dark woods of chairs and tables, and its shadows, and the women, and the leader who was coming to me. It had been so real, so vivid, and now it was all gone.

I awoke, desolate.

Come back! Or let me go back to you.

The room was gone, and the women with it, and she had not come yet, the leader, the queen, the mother, the Woman. An archetype, surely; but vanished before I could welcome her, before she could bring her message.

Night after night I tried to dream that dream again, tried to summon up the women and their leader. As I fell asleep, I would call out to them from within me, Come back. But they never returned.

At last I said to myself, I have the memory of the dream. I can work with that, study its signs, make it yield its meaning.

But that was a doomed effort. After all, wasn't that the very point of the dream? At the crossroads in my life, my guide, unlike Dante's, *didn't* come. All I had was a promise of a future coming.

So that was the meaning of my numinous dream: don't make a decision. How do you *not* make a decision?

If I went on to study for a Ph.D., that was a decision. If I *didn't* go on, that was also a decision.

A dilemma.

There was another way of examining my dream, that is, to look at the feelings aroused by the dream.

How had I felt?

First, discomfort and uneasiness at the noisy, crowded party.

Then, dislocation, when I discovered myself in that dark, empty room; and the tiny electric flickers of anxiety as I realized I didn't know how to find my way back.

Surprise at the arrival of the women.

And, most powerful of all, great anticipation of the arrival of the Woman, desire and waiting and readiness to welcome her, and a feeling of great peace in the waiting.

So there it was, not the meaning of the dream perhaps, but its message: peaceful waiting.

Which I took to mean that I would make no commitment, that I wouldn't decide either to take the Ph.D. or to leave it. I would go on as I was, I would continue with my studies, but without a decisive commitment to future action.

Does that make sense?

Even today I don't know. I went on wrestling for years with the dream. Who was this leader of the women, for whom I was waiting? She was alternatively the archetype of Woman, the feminine principle inside myself, my *anima,* the archetype of Mother, Mary, Mother of God, Queen of Heaven and of Earth, she was—who?

I suppose the deepest truth is that she is me, coming to myself; but meanwhile, she was all of these meanings I have suggested. After all, she remains, not an answer, but a question, a powerful and ongoing question, a *koan,* a riddle beyond sense and logic.

For a long time I clung to the promise, to the sense that I was waiting for something imminent. But gradually even that faded, and I went on with the usual business of life.

Which was demanding enough.

Hofstra had been a high-powered shock to me at first, but I had quickly gained confidence there. C. W. Post had been a place where I made several good friends, and almost effortlessly was an outstanding student. Stony Brook was something else again. All the doctoral graduate students here were hotshots. And young. I felt not only out of my league, but also *old.*

My first seminar was an ambitious one.

The eighteenth century is usually described in a shorthand kind of way as the Age of Reason. It is perhaps best characterized by the *philosophe* Voltaire, who detested irrationality, sentimentality, and God, not necessarily in that order. Cleverness—wit, precision, style, detachment, satire, elegance—was particularly valued in the eighteenth century.

But that is only a partial view.

It was also the age in which lunatic asylums first came into being. Up until the eighteenth century, crazy people wandered at will, occasionally revered as holy, generally left alone. Only if they bothered other people were they given special attention, such as being thrown into prison. In the eighteenth century, for the first time, madmen and madwomen assumed a category and a dwelling place all their own. Madness, in fact, cast its shadow over the entire century. It is notewor-

thy how many writers, great and near-great, William Blake, for example, and Christopher Smart, were mad, or nearly so, at frequent
intervals. Jonathan Swift died a madman. So that was the rationale of
the seminar, that the same white light of reason which burned so
clearly and so brightly also cast the blackest of shadows, in which
lurked exploitation, mass drunkenness, uninhibited violence, and
madness.

The seminar was a lively one. The rational qualities of cleverness,
elegance, and wit; the precise use of words; a certain detachment and a
"cool" stance—all of which characterized the century—were equally
valued in our class discussions. I remember how exasperated and angry
I would get at what I saw as scholarly escapism—my class members'
refusal to take sides, their refusal to become excited and emotional,
even passionate, about issues and opinions. Detachment to me was a
kind of withdrawal, a sterility. And yet that anger and exasperation
must have remained locked up inside me, and publicly I must have
displayed my intellectual weapons, old, formidable friends that they
were, because my friend James recalls me from that seminar as very
bright, highly intelligent, and also highly contrived and artificial.
Those words may sound pejorative; but in the context both of the
eighteenth century and of graduate school, they were qualities to be
sought after and cultivated. Contrived and artificial, after all, both
describe something not natural and untidy, but civilized and crafted. I
was, he says, a woman of artifice and reserve.

I, in my turn, remember James above anything else for his words.
How *abstract* I was, he says now about himself, with regret. But I
thought he was amazing. When James began to talk, gorgeous castles
of words spun into existence in the air, all turreted and pinnacled and
glittering.

And the things he said! I didn't know that what I was hearing was
philosophy. I only knew that his words, his ideas, his theoretical con-
structs bore no relation to the boring lectures I had absorbed and
regurgitated for one endless semester at Wellesley. But what James
talked of most was actually theology, which was a word beyond my
acquaintance. I would even have been hard put to define theology. All

I knew was that the things James talked about sparked my imagination, excited and stimulated me. So we two made our first tentative approaches at friendship, a friendship of words and ideas between a young Irish Catholic man of nearly thirty, a former seminarian, gay, and a Jewish wife and mother of forty, very sophisticated and worldly and sheltered and naive all at once, an odd couple in many ways.

There's a current expression I like a lot: what goes around, comes around. There's another way of putting it, as in psychotherapist Sheldon Kopp's book, *Even a Stone Can Be a Teacher:* "It has always been clear in myths and fairy tales that to flee from a prophecy is to make it come true."

And so it was for me.

Back in 1952, when I graduated from high school, my parents and teachers and relatives and friends all prophesied it: you will be an English teacher.

But I would not. I loved English. But I balked at doing women's work, and at being told what I would do, so, at that early crossroads, I chose to go to Wellesley and major in economics, and went out into the wide, wide masculine world of Wall Street, as far away as I could from teaching and English and imagination. Do you remember Robert Frost's poem, "The Road Not Taken"? This is how it begins:

> Two roads diverged in a yellow wood,
> And sorry I could not travel both
> And be one traveler, long I stood
> And looked down one as far as I could
> To where it bent in the undergrowth;
>
> Then took the other, . . .

I was not even sorry I could not travel both.

I took the other path without regret, certain that it would change my destiny. After all, that's what the end of Frost's poem promises:

> Two roads diverged in a wood, and I—
> I took the one less traveled by,
> And that has made all the difference.

I expected my decision to make all the difference. As if it did, as if it could. . . .

At Stony Brook, as at most universities, hapless freshmen innocently expect to be taught by the eminent names those universities boast of in their catalogs and public relations. Instead, they often get graduate students pressed into service at pitiful stipends teaching beginning courses without any qualifications or previous experience.

I'm sure it had been mentioned when I enrolled, but somehow it came as a big shock to me to realize that my fate had caught up with me.

I had once stood at a crossroads in a yellow wood, and chosen one of two divergent paths.

Years later, what had I found? That both paths had led to the same place.

Come September at Stony Brook, I was going to be an English teacher.

God at a Traffic Light

FRIEND OF MINE WHO, among his many occupations, is a college professor, is convinced that the cardinal sin a teacher can commit is to be boring. I'd do anything except stand on my head not to bore my students, he says. And adds thoughtfully, I guess I'd even stand on my head, too, if I thought they'd find it interesting, and learn something from it.

That's how I felt about the first class I ever taught, that fall semester of 1975. I would have jumped through fiery hoops for them. I gave them everything I had, everything I never even knew I had. Because, as everyone had predicted, I loved teaching.

And I loved that class. A few were very bright, a few very dull, the rest were scattered along the continuum between the poles.

A typical, average, ordinary classful of kids, except, presumably, to their mothers.

And to me.

Of course my students didn't know that they were my first class, didn't know that a lot of my exuberance in the first weeks was a mix of genuine excitement and nervous terror, that I had to take several deep breaths before making my entrance (and I always made an entrance, you didn't catch *me* meekly hanging around the desk waiting for my students to trickle in), that my hands shook for a few minutes at the beginning of each period so that I made sure not to handle note cards until I'd settled down, that I agonized over every comment I penciled in on their papers, every grade I gave them.

It's hard to believe that I could forget that first, special class, but there it is. I have a few hazy memories of my students, that's all. I had always presumed that my own high school and college teachers would remember me forever. Oh, well, another illusion down the tubes.

January 1976 brought a new semester, a new freshman composition class to teach, and a new seminar for me to attend, Medieval Drama. I was a veteran medievalist, so this seminar, too, would be fine, all smooth sailing, right?

Wrong.

For the first time since returning to school, I found myself involved in a class I hated. The class didn't begin that way, of course, with my hating it, although it did begin in a place of some unease for me. It began in a church. More precisely, in a churchyard.

Quem quaeritis? Where are you going?

Those are the words spoken by an angel to the grieving women on their way to the tomb, hurrying to retrieve the body of their beloved rabbi for a proper ritual burial after his shameful death on a cross.

The women respond, and there it is, the first dialogue in Western drama (according to prevailing theory), born in a churchyard, where some innovative priests vividly brought to life the gospel story of the Resurrection for their illiterate peasant-parishioners by means of an Easter sepulcher "play."

Once released, the spirit of play spread rapidly. Bible stories, from the Hebrew Scriptures and the gospels alike, crammed full of comedy and tragedy, action and emotion, all were dramatized: the creation of Adam and Eve; murderous Cain and blameless Abel; Abraham's obedient sacrifice of Isaac; the annunciation to Mary; the nativity of Jesus; raging Herod and the slaughter of the innocents; the bloody events of the Passion; Christ's harrowing of Hell; his Resurrection; and the grand and glorious finale, Judgment Day, good souls this way, bad souls that, descending into Hellmouth amid thunderous applause. All these dramas took their turn before the audience, set against their three-level backdrop of Earth, Heaven, and Hell.

Add to these events the sheer artistry of skillful verse, and you have the genius of medieval drama.

So what was wrong?

What was there for me to hate in the seminar?

The "so what?" of it, the reason why these plays were written and presented. Oh, the main thrust behind the plays is a worthy one: to teach an illiterate population the events of the Bible and of Christ's life and death, and thereby mirror to them the meaning of their own lives, and their right relationship to God. Don't scorn as primitive, either, the resources of this early theater: handwritten records remain of lavish expenditures for costumes, wigs, scenery, and special effects, of which gaping Hellmouths belching smoke and flames were the most spectacular. Everyone from miles around must have come to these great events! And been duly edified and entertained.

And taught, as corollary, to hate and despise and scorn the perfidious Jews.

From my point of view, a significant consequence of the plays, if not the main purpose of them, was the teaching of anti-Semitism, theologically and by example. As soon as one comes to the gospel stagings, most particularly the Passion plays, one is smacked in the face with the Jew as hypocrite, liar, cheat, murderer. Villains all. Comic villains, too, caricatures, figures of fun, but no less evil for all that.

Item: so many pence for red wigs and beards for Judas and all others, Pharisees, high priests, crowds.

Red fright wigs, hooked noses, the enemy. The forces of the devil.

All the elaborate costumes, ingenious staging, beautiful verse, all comes to a head in this: condemn the Jews.

I was brought up on stories of European pogroms in which Jews were beaten and killed and raped, their houses set on fire. To read these plays and imagine their staging, and the state of mind into which their audiences were put, was outrageous. *Here* were the seeds of the massacres of the Jews in medieval York and in Lincoln, of their expulsion from England. This stuff, like the Good Friday liturgy of the Church which has resulted in violence committed against Jews by zealous Christian neighbors, has been the instrument of horror and torture, even genocide. The modern Holocaust has deep, deep roots, and literature and liturgy, play and art are not innocent activities, but have consequences in the world.

Reading my assignments, I burned with anger and impotence.

How could our professor, himself a German Jew and a refugee from Nazi Germany, bring himself to teach this course? Make this exquisite *filth* his subject of specialization? I could not imagine how I could possibly write an acceptable midterm paper on the cycle plays.

Furthermore, when it came to my own Judaism, compared to what I knew of Christian theology and history, I felt my own ignorance. Because the vast majority of English literature up until the eighteenth century is, willy-nilly, also Christian literature, and because almost all of my studies fell into that time frame, I had become a highly educated (in a selective kind of way) Christian scholar. As a Jew I had the kind of learning that comes by osmosis. But it amounted to a child's knowledge of my own religion, which fueled my feelings of vulnerability and powerlessness before what I experienced as attacks on my people and my faith.

Perhaps it was my awareness of my own ignorance that prompted me to say yes rather than no to an unexpected telephone call.

I'd like to welcome you, said the woman's voice, on behalf of the Sisterhood, and to invite you—

Thinking ahead several years to Jane's bat mitzvah, we had joined our neighborhood Reform temple, but, since she wouldn't begin afterschool studies until September, I'd forgotten all about the temple until then.

I'd like to invite you, she went on, in a bubbly, cheery sort of voice, to come to our Tuesday morning adult education class. Are you interested?

I was an intellectual snob through and through, and in the normal course of events, I would (politely) have refused this prospect of amateur study. But things weren't normal, and I saw this as a heaven-sent chance to remedy my crippling ignorance.

And so I said Yes to her.

Rabbi Adam Gelb was a wonderful teacher. Brilliant, passionate about Judaism and about learning, he was the perfect antidote to those poisonous caricatures in the cycle plays.

Adam was himself a type of a prophet, fiery, certain, intolerant, inspired, and he taught us the prophets, beginning with Amos, who defended himself to a hostile Amaziah, the priest of Bethel, thus:

> I am no prophet, nor a prophet's son, but I am a herdsman and a dresser
> of sycamore trees, and the Lord took me from following the flock, and
> the Lord said to me, "Go, prophesy to my people Israel."

You see, said Adam, there were professional prophets, but Amos wasn't one, he was an amateur, unlearned, called by God for no reason that he could see. And he said, Why me? But then he did it.

As did Hosea, and Micah.

But Jonah was different. He was my favorite prophet.

> Now the word of the Lord came to Jonah the son of Amittai saying,
> "Arise, go to Nineveh, that great city, and cry against it; for their
> wickedness has come up before me." But Jonah rose to flee to Tarshish
> from the presence of the Lord.

God spoke to Jonah, and Jonah ran away.

He jumped on a ship to escape from God's command, but a terrible storm arose, a storm that Jonah knew arose from his presence, so that he resignedly ordered the sailors to throw him overboard, whence he was swallowed alive by a great fish, and only after spending three days and three nights in the fish's belly did Jonah grudgingly agree to obey God's command and go prophesy to Nineveh.

Which he did, with such success that the whole great city repented, and God changed his mind and did not destroy Nineveh.

And Jonah, whose prophesying had produced such a drastic conversion, what about him? Did he rejoice? Hardly.

It displeased Jonah exceedingly, and he was angry.

I guess he felt like a fool.

He went out of the city and sat under a tree and sulked, and didn't let go of his anger until God taught him about repentance and forgiveness and compassion in a personal way, by means of a vine that lived and died for Jonah.

A prophet after my own heart, my own wayward, stubborn, rebellious, disobedient heart.

On those satisfying Tuesday mornings, I would drive home stimulated and exhilarated by the joy of learning about people and things that mattered, that made sense to me.

And then, one Tuesday morning, something happened, something that didn't make sense at all, but simply *was,* against all intellect and all reason.

God spoke to me.

At a traffic light.

I hate even to write these words, outrageous, absurd, nonsensical words.

And yet that's exactly what happened.

It's a good thing that the car wasn't in motion. I was stopped at a traffic light, nothing different or unusual, my ordinary route home. Suddenly there was light all around me, a brilliant blinding white light that filled everything and everywhere—there was only light, nothing else remained—and a voice spoke from the depths of me, though I heard it as a voice coming from outside. I'm *not* crazy, you know, I'm perfectly aware that there was no voice that anyone else would have heard if they'd been in the car, and yet the voice was perfectly clear to

me, the voice from inside that sounded from outside, and it spoke
words that weren't exactly words, and this is what it said:

You will never have to be alone again. I will be with you always. If
you wish—

Oh my God!

My heart leaped like a fish to the bait, to the promise, with a
longing I wasn't even aware that I felt. In that instant I experienced
the loneliness of my whole lifetime, my longing for a companion, my
second self, my soul's completion. Oh, those are all phrases I can say
now, then it was only longing, yearning that flooded over me. Yes, I
longed to say in those first few instants, oh, yes, I want that, I want
you, and then the terror washed over me.

Sheer terror, and shame, and unworthiness.

How could I think of such a thing, how could I even long for it, it
would be unbearable to be in God's company, God's eye on me always, seeing all the shoddiness, the deceits, the meanness and the
ugliness; I couldn't stand that. (That wasn't God's judgment on me,
you understand. It was my judgment, the promise become a threat.)

It wasn't possible.

No, I said in the depths of me. No sound, my lips didn't move, I
don't mean anything like that. Just no, I said, or thought, or felt.

The light faded, and the traffic light was green, and I turned the
corner and continued driving home in the most ordinary way.

But even before I completed the right turn I knew that I was sorry,
that I had given the wrong answer, had missed the opportunity.

God, I wanted to say, I'm sorry. I changed my mind.

But I couldn't, any more than I could have said yes to that incredi-
ble promise. So what I really felt on the rest of the drive home, two
minutes perhaps, was how sorry I was that I couldn't say yes, but not
in a sad way. I felt, actually, an extraordinary calm and peacefulness.

I was, all of a sudden, very clear. I wished I could have said yes, oh,
I *wished* it with all my heart, but I didn't regret my no, because, for
once, I truly saw and understood myself. I was simply too afraid. It was
not possible for me.

And I accepted that about myself, accepted the fear, and the truth, and didn't blame myself.

And didn't really feel sad.

What I felt was *alive* in a way that I had never experienced before, an intensity—I still have no words for it, nor concepts, even.

It was simply *what happened*.

The light, that blinding light, had vanished swiftly from the intersection and the traffic light. But somehow it had irradiated my heart and even my refusal didn't darken the light.

I was happy. Happy!

Not Whee, this is wonderful! Nothing like that.

Satisfied with what was, satisfied and content with the offer, with the refusal.

I lived for weeks in the happiness and the amazement.

Obviously I didn't tell anyone about my experience. I knew better than that. Who would believe me? *I* wouldn't have believed me.

And yet, stubborn as Jonah, I clung to the truth of my experience. That really happened, I would say to myself. It doesn't matter how crazy it sounds. *It really happened*.

And often I wanted to say, Come back, God, I changed my mind, I'm ready now. But God didn't come back, any more than the women in my dream ever returned. And, in any event, I knew better. I hadn't changed my mind. I was still afraid, nothing had changed about me at all.

Time passed, the memory began to fade. The world went right on being as it was. The world generally does. Besides, even though I've used pages of words to try and convey some idea to you of what happened, in fact the entire incident probably took thirty seconds.

Thirty seconds! What can possibly happen in thirty seconds?

So I thought I was still the same.

Earthquakes don't take long, either, to alter a landscape permanently.

I didn't have the knowledge or understanding then that would have enabled me to see how actually ordinary, or, at least *traditional,* what had happened to me really was. Light? Light is a symbol of the divine in almost every religion. Voices? Christians see visions, Christ resurrected, for instance, but Jews hear voices. Moses, Elijah, Saul become Paul, they all heard voices. There is even a name for Jewish revelation: *Bat Kol.* The Daughter of the Voice. And the burning bush, the one Moses saw in the desert, the bush that burned but was not consumed? A fire-red traffic light, when you come right down to it, is actually a pretty accurate, if comical, twentieth-century translation of a burning bush. All of the elements of my experience were, well, *commonplace.*

Yet somehow I *wasn't* the same. Something in me had been set on fire, the heart, the soul, the true self. Whatever it's called, that had been set alight, became fuel burning on a perpetual altar, an eternal flame that I had no power to blow out, although, God knows, in the years that followed I wanted to and tried to hard enough. It propelled me, the light, the fire. I became a seeker.

Later I would experience it as hunger, and thirst, and emptiness, but it began as restlessness. The seeking began simply as restlessness. What was I seeking? I wanted—I didn't know what, but I knew I wanted—*something.*

You have made us for yourself, O God, and our hearts will never rest until they rest in you.

Years later, well after I had found, or been found, I heard that saying of St. Augustine for the first time, and finally understood what I had been seeking from that moment in 1976 when I stopped at a traffic light, the world ended, and the world began.

Another Book About Zen?

*I*T WOULD BE PLEASANT TO THINK that my encounter with the mystical traffic signal had lit a strong and steady blaze within me. But it wouldn't be true.

I went on living my life, just as I had been.

I continued the Tuesday morning adult education classes, where, in the fall of 1976, Rabbi Gelb tackled the book of Genesis, in the beginning.

Bereshit barah Elohim . . .

"First of all, God made . . ."

The heavens and the earth, and all that is within them, and man and woman, twice he made them, once in poetry, as equals in creation, and once in narrative form as a superior and a subordinate.

God made human beings in his image, you see, and man returned the compliment right there in the opening chapter of God's story by creating a sexist god in his own image, an oppressor-god, who plays favorites and sets arbitrary limits, and categorizes, a distorted god in whom I no longer believe, because that god is not the real thing. The real thing is the Creator, the One Who, in the beginning, in the first version we encounter, made us thus:

> So God created man in his own image, in the image of God created he him; male and female created he them. And God blessed them, and God said unto them, Be fruitful, and multiply, and replenish the earth, and subdue it: and have dominion over the fish of the sea, and over the fowl of the air, and over every living thing that moveth upon the earth.

Mutually he blessed them, mutually empowered them.

The moment of mutuality—

Which vanishes in the very next chapter, where we meet Adam and Eve and the snake, and the next thing you know, we screw it up. Not *her,* Eve. *We* screw it up, Adam, Eve, the scribe, you, me. The story, set in motion, hurtles headlong, Cain and Abel and murder, and Noah and the flood—time flies in Genesis—and then we're there in Ur of the Chaldees, with a man called Abraham and his wife Sarah.

And Sarah was barren. She had no child.

The deepest curse possible upon a Jewish woman, sign of divine disfavor, grounds for divorce. Her single sacrament dishonored, the barren woman receives reproach in the community, reproach, and pity, and humiliation.

I should know. I've been there.

And so, to my astonishment, were all those great women, the matriarchs of Israel, Sarah, Rebecca, Rachel, all barren until God intervened, a prominent theme and motif in Genesis, this barrenness, a sign, our young rabbi taught us, that it is God who rules the mysteries of life, God who insures the continuance of his people, God who determines the patrimony, God, and not the activities or desires of humankind.

Those women would know just how I felt, then, these Mothers who first were barren: and so, studying the matriarchs of my people began a healing of one of my deepest wounds.

The rabbi covered ground quickly: we studied the binding of Isaac, the story of God's demand of Abraham that he sacrifice his son, and of

Abraham's obedience, for which he was so praised by God and Jews and Christians (but not by me); and Exodus, and Chronicles, and the book of the sufferings of Job, and, as the year rolled around, ended and began again, we covered the books of the women, the stories of the convert Ruth, and Esther the heroine (for whom I was named), and Deborah, warrior-judge in Israel. And then we studied *Pirke Avoth, The Wisdom of the Fathers,* a classical text which is the abstract and philosophical teachings of the early rabbis on the meaning and values and significance of life, and the proper ways to live it. And we also studied, before the rabbi left for his own pulpit, a little bit of Psalms and Proverbs, with emphasis on the form and structure of the Hebrew language, and the characteristic repetitive patterns of Hebrew poetry.

When Adam Gelb left, Rabbi Joshua Rothstine arrived to succeed him as assistant rabbi. They were two different types, each admirable and talented in his own way: Adam, brilliant, inspired, aloof; Joshua, warm, open, impulsive. Adam was my teacher; Joshua became my friend.

With Joshua we studied the prayer book, its structure and forms. I already knew how to read Hebrew, to daven a little—that is, to pray the prayers aloud. Now I learned something about *what* I was praying, where and when it originated, and why the prayers were combined in the order in which they are, a matter of such importance that the prayer book is actually called in Hebrew a *siddur,* meaning, "that which is set in order."

Simultaneously I was continuing the rest of my lives.

In the fall of 1976, I took my final course at Stony Brook, in Renaissance Drama. From then on, my studies were individual directed reading in preparation for a three-hour comprehensive oral examination. I continued teaching. And, as always, my *real life* went on: my life as wife and mother at home, with parent-teacher conferences, car pools, cooking, shopping, birthday parties, Jewish holidays, the daily round.

Routine.

Not so routine was Frank's growing unhappiness with the changing corporate climate at Merrill Lynch. In his first years at Merrill Lynch there was still enough freewheeling innovative spirit remaining from the founding years of Charlie Merrill to make for a challenging and spirited atmosphere. But then came a palace revolution won by the time-study men, the managers. Being a Merrill Lynch account executive meant an increasingly gray existence. Individuals were ground down, grist for the corporate mill, to make things neat and tidy for the company.

First Frank chafed, and then he, my mild-mannered husband, most amiable of men, began to seethe inside. Wall Street brokers have stressful jobs normally; they notoriously suffer either from ulcers or a bad back. The muscles in Frank's back began to spasm with increasing frequency.

Many of the men from his training-school class had already left to join a regional, Philadelphia-based investment firm, Butcher & Singer.

Inevitably, Frank was approached to leave Merrill and come to Butcher & Singer. The first few times, he said no. He was afraid I would be upset at the insecurity of his starting all over again, no guarantees.

He was right. The prospect scared me. After all, he was doing nicely at Merrill Lynch. We lived pretty much as we wanted to, far from rich, but comfortable. We had something to lose, all right, if he changed jobs.

But he was so unhappy!

The price of security was simply too high. We could manage, I said, and crossed my fingers behind my back.

And so, in April 1976, sixteen years older than when he'd started, Frank began again: the long hours, the Saturdays, the cold calls, the mail and phone campaigns. It wasn't easy. Once again we faced uncertainty of income, an unknown future.

But over against that was Frank's visibly becoming a new man; or, rather, the old man, good-natured, funny, thoughtful, reemerged, with new qualities added, a sense of freedom, of confidence and competence, of increasing strength.

When it came to doing anything around the house, however, he was the same old Frank. So was I. Do-it-yourself for us meant we used our own fingers to walk through the Yellow Pages to find the experts who would come and rescue us, repair our faucets, oil burner, washer, dryer. You name it, we didn't fix it. The insides of machines baffled and bored us both.

Frank sometimes felt guilty about being so unhandy, he felt un-macho, almost un-American. But me? It was feminine, even charming, to be helpless in the presence of machinery of any kind. Men were *expected* to rescue helpless women from mechanical mishaps.

And I was lucky enough to have Ben Shor, Your Appliance Repair Man, as my chief rescuer.

One didn't get Ben Shor out of the Yellow Pages. He was a hidden treasure, passed on by word of mouth through affluent Long Island neighborhoods of non-do-it-yourselfers. Ben came to the houses of lots of people I knew, but only if he liked you. Which meant, really, only if you were willing to listen to him, and to enter into a rather lopsided dialogue. Ben was a balding homespun philosopher in a baggy boiler-suit, a genuine certified eccentric, with opinions, mostly contrary to prevailing notions, about everything under the sun.

Ben obviously moonlighted from some other job. First of all, you never got Ben himself, you always had to leave a message for him.

So you'd leave your message. And then you'd wait.

In the meantime, you'd go to the laundromat, eat at a restaurant or bring in Chinese, depending on the problem. You'd wait, and you'd wonder. This time, is he going to come? And then, a day or three or four later, usually when you were just about to sit down to dinner, the doorbell would ring, and there he'd be, doctor fix-it with his little bag of tools and his duck-billed fishing cap. He'd inspect the latest problem, fix it, then announce his fee, but only after being asked, just as a fine restaurant will never bring you a check unless you request it. Ben's fees were absurd. Seven dollars, twelve-fifty, fifteen tops.

Once, in response to a washing machine emergency, Ben appeared out of the night. As usual, I preceded him down to the basement, fluttering my hands in charming feckless feminine fashion—oh, I just can't imagine what's wrong this time—

Ben was so quick upon this occasion that I hadn't even slipped away upstairs before he straightened up and announced that the washer was fixed. Indigestion, from eating a sock. I was amazed, and shook my head, marveling at his expertise. Ben leaned against the washing machine, and in his slow rather nasal drawl said to me, There's a book you really ought to read, because you're right there in the book. You, to the life.

Oh!

I was kind of flattered.

Here was this extraordinarily competent person reading a book and thinking about *me* in response to some character who, in my vanity, I was sure was charming, or interesting, or witty, or funny, or—

What's the name of the book? I asked eagerly. And what character?

Don't worry, said Ben. You'll recognize yourself, right in the first few pages. The book is called *Zen and the Art of Motorcycle Maintenance*.

I went out the next day, found it in paperback, brought it home and began eagerly to read. I recognized myself right away, right there in the first four or five pages. Unfortunately, I wasn't charming *or* interesting *or* witty *or* funny. Or even feminine. But it was recognizably *me,* the man who bought an expensive motorcycle with no interest, inclination, or intention of maintaining it, a foolish incompetent who turned over his responsibilities, his mobility, and his safety to others, refused even to attempt to use the faculties and qualities with which he was born, faculties of seeing and reasoning, qualities of courage and willingness to risk.

Not a pretty picture I saw in that mirror held up to me by Ben Shor.

I read the whole long book, slow going it was in places, and emerged from my motorcycle journey across country with Robert Pirsig and his young son in a kind of dazed amazement.

What possibilities he was talking about!

That I might see for myself, decide for myself, without permission, without protectors and guides and rescuers, do-it-myself. Live my life by myself.

To do with my hands, to make and shape and tinker. My shock at such possibilities showed me clearly what kind of an abstract world I had been living in, a world where ideas excluded things, theory excluded being, where I lived in my head rather than in the hard-edge "outside." No wonder child-rearing was often difficult for me. If there's one thing children are, it's concrete.

The reality of shitty diapers—

There is a Hasidic saying: when the student is ready, the teacher will come. But not all teachers are flesh and blood. Often enough they are sheets of folded paper held in cardboard binders; but, as if alive, they somehow leap off the bookshelf to attract your attention.

Here I am!

And so two teachers came to me at this time. I read both of them avidly, thirstily; and over the following years reread them, each time absorbing something new from my teacher. One of them was theoretical, abstract, philosophical. The other, who taught the same lessons, did so by means of story.

All these years I had retained my interest in mystery stories, so, appropriately, one of my teachers was a mystery writer named Janwillem Van de Wetering. When I ran out of his mystery novels, on a whim I tackled the card catalog to see what else I could find by him. And I found another book, a nonfiction book, but with an intriguing title: *The Empty Mirror*. It was subtitled, *Experiences in a Zen Monastery*.

Synchronicity? The Torah adage in action, what I tell you two times is true? I read *The Empty Mirror,* finished it, and immediately began reading it again. It is an account of a little more than a year in the life of the Dutch author when he was a restless, questing young man. It reads like a novel, with absorbing characters, enigmatic vignettes, stories within stories, and always the mounting suspense of the drama, Will the young man achieve the enlightenment he seeks?

The ultimate importance of the book for me, I think, is that in the end he did *not* succeed, he left the monastery in Kyoto without *satori,* without ever looking into the empty mirror.

And yet he did not fail.

There is no sense of failure in *The Empty Mirror*. It is a joyful book, bursting with life. He did it, you see. He went to Japan, entered the Zen Buddhist monastery, lived there, met the people, heard the stories, did the sitting, did the work, endured.

So he wasn't enlightened!

Nevertheless, he did it. Lived it. The way of Zen.

Not the fruit of action, but the *action* of action. Just *do* it, he taught.

About this same time, I encountered my other teacher, the Tibetan Buddhist Chogyam Trungpa, in the pages of *The Myth of Freedom and the Way of Meditation*.

The Myth of Freedom and the Way of Meditation was another mirror for me, not an empty mirror, but one full of faults I immediately recognized as my own: self-absorption, passion, stupidity, meanness of spirit. It was like glimpsing the dark side of the moon, the me nobody knew . . . including myself, because that me was always turned away, always hidden from view.

But now I knew I wasn't unique, or alone in that darkness.

These are conditions, Trungpa taught, in calm, measured prose, that afflict everyone who lives in illusion and unreality. It's okay. That's just the way it is.

The real world about which he taught contradicted everything I had spent my life learning from my parents, my teachers, my temples, the Declaration of Independence, and the founding fathers. Success? Perfection? The pursuit of happiness? Chogyam Trungpa's world was filled with *dukkha,* pain and suffering, disappointment and death. *And I did not find it depressing.* On the contrary, I found it exhilarating, because, while it was certainly dark and bleak, it rang true to me, it affirmed my perceptions, and thereby I found a first measure of— freedom.

Oh.

I could stop smiling. Stop trying to be wonderful, and perfect, and good.

That was the promise of Chogyam Trungpa: that one could come to see clearly the reality of things, of pain and suffering, disappointment and death.

I had, in fact, already read books by two authors who presented a world as dark and unrelieved as this, James T. Farrell and Mary Mc-Carthy. I was drawn to their books, stark, grim, especially McCarthy's account of her scarifying childhood and her bitter unhappiness, because I recognized that they were the truth, no sugar coating, no cosmetics, no masks.

But I thought (can you credit this?) that kind of truth, that kind of reality, was for Catholics or Buddhists only. Only *their* world was that way. (And my feelings were that way.) My world was different, sunlit, rational, abounding with happy endings. All you had to do was keep trying, harder and harder. Didn't everybody tell me so?

Yet here was Chogyam Trungpa telling me that the dark vision belonged to everybody, that I was entitled to it, that I could if I tried someday glimpse the truth in the dark, empty mirror.

The way to that truth was by meditation, which meant sitting.

Just sitting?

Like Janwillem had done in the Zen monastery in Japan, hour after hour after hour, until his tortured legs made him sick with pain?

That's not for me.

And yet—the appeal of sitting still, of becoming quiet, empty, of letting go, oh, that was a great appeal.

Chogyam Trungpa spelled out the way, in this long passage which I copied into a little notebook and carried around with me, copying it into successive notebooks, for years, without being able to imagine a time when I would have the courage to embark upon it:

This path begins formally with the student taking refuge in the buddha, the dharma and the sangha—that is, in the lineage of teachers, the teachings and the community of fellow pilgrims. We expose our neurosis to our teacher, accept the teachings as the path and humbly share our confusion with our fellow sentient beings. Symbolically, we leave our homeland, our property and our friends. We give up the familiar ground that supports our ego, admit the helplessness of ego to control its world and secure itself. We give up our clingings to superiority and self-preservation. But taking refuge does not mean becoming dependent upon our teacher or the community or the scriptures. It means giving up searching for a home, becoming a refugee, a lonely person who must depend upon himself. A teacher or fellow traveler or the scriptures might show us where we are on a map and where we might go from there, but we have to make the journey ourselves. Fundamentally, no one can help us.

If we seek to relieve our loneliness, we will be distracted from the path. Instead, we must make a relationship with loneliness until it becomes aloneness.

That'll teach me to reject God's offered companionship, I thought bitterly. *Now* look what I'll have to do!

I could recognize an authentic teaching when I heard it, but I oscillated between desiring and fearing to set out on this new way. I hungered to know more about it, though, and so I started haunting the library, hunting systematically through the shelves: Philip Kapleau's *The Three Pillars of Zen; Zen Flesh, Zen Bones; Zen Mind, Beginner's Mind;* anything and everything, books by the armful, voracious hungry ghost, until one day my son John, exasperated and irritated by my absorption, burst out, "Another book about *Zen?*"

Nine years old, my son, the guru.

The scorn of his tone of voice.

He was right, essentially. Just *do it!*

But it was all necessary, all the reading, all the thinking, all the wondering, all the wanting and the not-wanting, all of it, every book about Zen.

It was my necessary next step.

I didn't know it, but I was on the way.

Giving Up, Giving Over

*Y*OU HAVE IT ALL, said the middle-aged woman in St. Louis, almost accusingly, after I had finished a speaking engagement there. I really envy you. You've got it all.

Oh, lady!

A sword in my heart, thrust and twist. Oh, lady, if you only knew.

Only a year before, I too had thought I had it all, not one brilliant career, but several, and nothing but promise shining on each.

In the academic world, I had come up with a dissertation idea that was actually practicable and useful, not common attributes of dissertations: a facsimile edition of the as-yet-uncollected letters of the poet John Donne.

This was *such* a good idea that one of my former professors even volunteered to help me apply for a grant of some kind to defray the costs of necessary research; and, at the beginning of 1978, I received a

$6,000 dissertation fellowship from the American Association of University Women for the academic year 1978–79.

But there was already something more exciting afoot than the fellowship. Studying for the comprehensive oral examination for the Ph.D. at Stony Brook had been a grueling ordeal, and after I passed in 1977 I was reluctant to begin work right away on the dissertation.

Why don't we take a trip? Frank said.

Where would we go?

Oh, I don't know, he said. How about Israel? Isn't the temple sponsoring a trip to Israel in May?

Oh, Israel, I said. That would mean flying for hours and hours, fifteen hours, isn't it? I'd never make it.

They'd have to carry me off the plane, I said, like *this*. And demonstrated, rigid seated posture, white knuckles, hands clenched.

Frank smiled.

Take a positive approach, he said. If you went on the temple trip it might be different, you could relax on the plane, you'd know people, maybe it would even be like Chaucer, people could tell stories. It would be fun. Like pilgrims.

And I looked at him, and a glint came into my eye, and something stirred in me. (You only need to know that the cantor at the temple in those days was named Bellink.)

You might have something, I said slowly. Just think, if the cantor led the trip, and people told stories, I could write them down, and we could call it—the Cantor Bellink Tales!

And Frank smacked his forehead and groaned in a satisfactory way, because I had neatly turned the tables on him. *He* is the master of the pun, and I am normally the one to groan.

We laughed together, and forgot about it.

Except that, the next morning, the idea awoke with me. And I decided that it was a pretty good idea. I got down my well-thumbed Chaucer from the shelf, reread the prologue to the *Canterbury Tales,* and started thinking about the medieval pilgrims who set out one April morning on horseback for Canterbury. There were a knight and

a monk and a prioress, a franklin and a cook, a shipman and a par-
doner. What could be more remote from the men and women I had
known in Roslyn, Great Neck, Brooklyn?

And yet—

The longer I allowed my mind to jog along with these pilgrims, the
more familiar they began to seem to me. Chaucer's pilgrims wore
different clothing, and their accents and their occupations were different; but at their core I knew them all, knew all these types from the
Jewish world that was my womb and matrix.

Was the bus Frank's idea or mine? I don't remember. But suddenly
there it was: a tour bus full of American Jews traveling through Israel,
visiting tourist sites, going to Jerusalem, and telling stories to pass the
time. *Jewish* stories.

And so a book came into being, a book of miracles. Getting an
agent was a miracle. Her auctioning it off to Simon & Schuster seemed
a miracle, its publication in 1979 and the speaking tours I was sent out
on were miracles. I was on top of the world.

So there were my achievements in what I still thought of as a man's
world. But I felt successful also in a woman's world, as a mother whose
daughter had finally achieved, albeit in a blizzard, her Jewish coming-
of-age. In January 1978 Jane had become a *bat mitzvah,* a daughter of
the covenant, the ritual title that had meant so much to me because it
had been denied to me all those long years ago.

Jane had redeemed my past.

I was also a wife, had been one for eighteen years, happy years, a
happy husband, a successful wife. And I was a friend, with many warm
and loving friends, some new, many of long-standing, a successful
friend. But who values these things, wife, friend?

Not society.

What do you *do?* What titles do you hold? What awards have you
received? How many people did you beat out for them? How much
money do you make?

Those are society's meaningful questions, the biggies.

And: how have your children turned out? What do *they* do? What grades do they get, what prizes, what jobs? All of which determines the answer to that other big, meaningful question, what kind of mother are you?

When's the last time you heard someone held up for honor this way: oh, she's a wonderful wife! He's a terrific husband! What a marvelous friend!

As the world sees it, then, so did I. No big deal.

Besides, they were natural, those roles. They came easy to me, like breathing. And anyone knows that if you don't have to make a big effort to do something, really work for it, then it's not worth a whole lot.

Where it *really* counted, in work and in mothering, I was well on my way.

And yet, within two years, those brilliant careers had tarnished, eroded, crumbled, fallen away to ashes, like Dead Sea fruit.

The first to go was my academic career.

In the winter of 1978, I made two research trips to Washington to work at the Folger Library on their holograph letters of John Donne.

It was on the second trip that a visiting professor with whom I was taking a coffee break remarked that he was sure he had read somewhere about just such an edition already announced by a famous scholar, now, who was it? he said. Oh, yes, it was Patrides, I'm *sure* it was Patrides, he said, he's doing an edition of John Donne's letters.

How can I tell you what it's like as a scholar to hear news like that? Maybe like arriving at the altar to be told that your prospective spouse is off someplace exchanging vows with somebody else. Or maybe it's as simple as getting kicked in the gut by a horse.

That news dimmed some vital spark.

My dissertation director argued strongly with me when I said I was abandoning the dissertation. That's silly, he said. It's not necessary. You can have the dissertation ready with ten letters as the model before Patrides even gets started on his edition, he said. It doesn't invalidate your dissertation.

But it did for me.

A four-year-old: if I can't be captain, I won't play. If I can't do the whole edition, I won't do anything.

And I didn't.

And that was how I became one of the vast army of A.B.D.'s, All-But-Dissertation graduate students. Failed scholars. Like failed priests. But I didn't care. I had other options. I was an *author.*

Going to Jerusalem was published in the spring of 1979.

In New York, except for one Barnes & Noble bookstore window, its publication was a nonevent.

No one ever reviewed it for the *New York Times.*

It not only didn't become a bestseller; it didn't even sell out its initial printing. No one wanted the paperback rights. Or movie rights.

Whether it was the breaks of the publishing game, or karma, whatever, it had become apparent by the end of 1979 that *Going to Jerusalem* was not going to make it big.

My editors and agent and husband weren't daunted. The breaks of the game, they all said. Now the *next* one, that'll make it, they said. They were eager, optimistic.

So how could I tell them, who believed in me so firmly, that I no longer believed in myself, that, just as with my dissertation, when my grandiose dreams and illusions were smashed, so were my courage and will and resolve. In my heart I abandoned the dream, abandoned the image of myself as author. I gave up.

I kept on writing. What else was there to do?

But increasingly the writing was an empty act, propelled by will-power, without my own self-cooperation, a great millstone to push, Sisyphus-like, uphill.

And increasingly I felt hollow.

An impressive facade, but hollow.

Painful as these failures were, it was the third failure that penetrated deepest, right to my heartspring, it felt like, and that was my failure as a mother.

I think that it was with Jane's bat mitzvah that the ghosts began to walk. Not her ghosts. Mine. Jane's bat mitzvah meant her coming-of-age, and her entrance into the fullness of her own riddling question, Who am I?

Which activated in me my own unexorcised demons, every unanswered question, every raw wound and suppressed desire of my own adolescent psyche.

Who am I?

If I don't know that, how can I know Jane?

There is a poem by Anne Sexton called "The Double Image," which in five lines lays out the drama for Jane and me, daughter and mother.

> I, who was never quite sure
> about being a girl, needed another
> life, another image to remind me.
>
> And this was my worst guilt: you could not cure
> nor soothe it. I made you to find me.

Adopted, not made: otherwise, an exact diagnosis.

Not an extraordinary story. One enacted daily in countless households across the country, an ordinary, banal story of mothers and daughters. But the pain and the suffering and the warping of lives are no less profound because it is so ordinary. An everyday tragedy is no less a tragedy.

And now I can hear my son, gravely offended.

Don't *I* count? Why is it always about Jane?

Whatever my shortcomings as a mother to my son, and there were a sufficiency of them, nonetheless our outlines were clear to us both. I was an adult, his mother, a woman, and he was a child, my son, a boy.

Mothers and daughters are different. The outlines become blurred for us. We become shape-shifters.

When Jane was first toddling, I would hold her hand and experience strange dislocations. Whose hand was big, whose was small, who was the mother, who the child?

What does it mean to be a mother, a daughter, a woman? All the meanings were there to be forged anew, to be made for myself out of my own observation and experience and responses. But all I knew were the patterns with which I had been raised, for better and for worse, patterns which I was bound to repeat, in a vain hope of perfecting them.

When Jane was little, I clung to the illusion that she was malleable, controllable, that I could *lick her into shape,* as the phrase has it, much as in Shakespeare's time there still lingered the folk wisdom that bears give birth to formless lumps and then use their rough tongues to lick those lumps into the shape of bear cubs. By my tongue, like Momma Bear, I could *talk* her into being, not only what I wanted her to be, but what I had absorbed as the blueprint of what she *should* be.

I needed Jane, needed her to be my container, to hold for me all my unfulfilled dreams, my desires and wishes and fears. This was my daughter, my self. I would relive my life through her, she would find me, I would at last *get it right.*

Even when Jane was little, it was apparent how strong-willed she was, how much her own self, how different from me. But parents have so much actual power over little children that for years I could sustain my illusion of shaping her as I chose, could cling to my projections as if they were the truth of my daughter.

As she grew to be nine and ten and eleven, I wonder how much I saw of *her* at all, and how much I saw my own fantasy self. Not until she was thirteen, however, was she able to jolt me awake.

I hate Hebrew school, I always hated it, and now that I finished my bat mitzvah, I'm never going back. I'm never setting foot in a temple again, and you can't make me.

Nor could we.

Out of nowhere. Nowhere? Out of all the words and grimaces and hangings-back that I had resolutely refused to heed, had smiled and talked out of existence.

That was the beginning of the refusals, one after the other; she refused any longer to be my container. She still mirrored me to myself, but what I saw now in her mirror was . . .

A changeling. Overnight my sweet docile little baby had been spirited away, and in her place appeared a defiant, outrageous girl-woman, whose only pleasure seemed to be to shock and flout and taunt me—cigarettes, pot, beer, staying out till all hours with kids who were, you know, not like us, different religion, different culture, different class. Every value I held Jane seemed to despise and trample on. The particulars aren't important. They belong to Jane, to her own story, and you can fill in any gaps with your own experience, or your cousin's or your neighbor's or your friend's, anyplace where there are teenagers and the trouble runs deep.

Teenage years are difficult anyway. The explosive ingredient here, I think, was my panic.

My own legacy of worry and anxiety and pessimism, my early warning system, went on alert. What will become of her? Whatever could be the worst possible thing, that was the vivid picture my imagination painted for me. And now I fell back on the only safety factor I knew, the legalistic concept of the *hedge,* guarding a prohibition by an additional prohibition, a concept I had myself rebelled against, but now made my own. The more Jane rebelled, the more new prohibitions I loaded on her. Soon every word that fell from my lips was yelling or accusation, No or Don't, frogs and toads, every encounter became a confrontation. Whatever perspective I had dwindled to vanishing point, until, implacable enemies, we locked horns constantly.

I had been so unhappy myself, I had resolved that things would be different for my daughter, she would find only acceptance and understanding and love. How had things turned out so badly?

A Jewish mother's curse on her difficult child is this: you should only grow up to have one just like you.

Die appeleh ne fallt far fun de bammeleh. The apple doesn't fall far from the tree.

An irresistible force, an immovable object.

In the spring of 1979, Jane began dating someone seriously. At fourteen! And he was Christian, this was a *shandah,* a scandal. Another concept I had myself detested and rebelled against; and now I used it as a line of defense against my daughter's actions, knowing no other way.

We sent her, unwilling, to a summer program on the grounds of

Wellesley College, and there, among the familiar hills and woods and Gothic buildings of my own college days, we visited her, stony-faced, a bandanna folded and tied around her forehead like a leftover child of the sixties, defiance in a red bandanna, and hints of wildness and danger, and yet, on the surface, everything seemed normal enough.

That same summer appeared to be my time of triumph, on promotion tours, making speeches, autographing books. For long periods of time I forgot my worries and anxieties about Jane. But in the night, when I would wake in a strange hotel room, they would descend upon me, a smothering blanket, a fist around my heart, constricting it.

You have it all, she had said to me, the middle-aged woman in St. Louis.

What I had was a telephone call from Frank.

Jane was arrested on Cape Cod, but don't worry, it's all straightened out now.

Frank had borne the brunt of it, the first shock. By the time I heard, half a continent away, the resolution had been reached.

And was it so terrible? It happens on the Cape, and on Fire Island, all the time. People, not just teenagers, arrested for holding a beer can exposed on the street. Two summers ago a woman was arrested on Fire Island for eating a cookie while standing on the sidewalk.

At the time it *was* so terrible, it was the worst thing I could imagine, my child a lawbreaker, a criminal, a disgrace.

Fall came, school began again. Jane continued her quarrel with the school, and with me, and with her life. We saw psychologists and guidance counselors and lived our waking nightmare.

And the wintry day finally arrived when I gave up.

Zen had become a part of my life. With the encouragement of my friend James I had begun sitting, nothing formal or fancy, just-sitting, every weekday morning, on the piano bench, sitting still for twenty minutes by the kitchen timer, with nothing happening, just sitting. During that fall, those twenty minutes were often my only respite from my daily insanity.

But latterly there was no peace anywhere. I sat, and tried to empty my mind, and my worries and fears bubbled up from deep within, and at last, one morning, instead of trying to banish my feelings, I allowed myself just this once to experience them, and as I did, something frozen within me gave way, dissolved in a weeping that was only inside, and the realization flooded over me, in horror, that I could no longer love Jane.

In that moment, I hated her.

The giving up of scholarship and of authorship had been about expectations, and disappointment of expectations, and the smashing of self-images. But in each of those I had made a choice to give up.

This giving up was not a choice. I *had* no choice. I *could not* do anything else. All my strength, my intelligence, willpower and discipline and experience—I had come to the limits of them, had run out my string.

I can no more.

Always before I had rushed to embrace failure voluntarily, so that I could escape the full humiliation, the real failure, the powerlessness.

I can no more.

This was the thing itself, bitter cup to the dregs, this is the truth and I am drowning in it.

And in that moment of utter despair, there was, astoundingly, a presence with me.

What I saw, I saw with my eyes closed, sitting in a quiet living room, an ordinary woman sitting alone on a piano bench.

But she was there.

I experienced her presence as a woman's, a huge figure all in black, seated, wrapped in a black cloak, a black shawl veiling her face so that I couldn't see it even if I had dared to look; but I didn't, because she glowed, that is the only way I can describe her, all in black as she was, glowing with an orange flame at the core of her, a hearth-mother, a vestal virgin. I had the crazy sense that this was somehow Mary, the Mother of us all, Virgin Mother; but she was not some porcelain doll all golden-haired and blue-eyed, this was a woman, a full and mature woman who had lived and suffered, fire within her, with an ample lap, not just for my daughter, but for me as well. I could be enfolded there in a corner of her shawl, wrapped in her warmth, and held, and comforted, and I knew that she was the answer to what I hadn't even known was a prayer, was the answer to what I was to do about Jane.

Take her, I said, without words.

Take my daughter, love her, hold her, care for her.

And she received her.

This great figure, this presence in black with the glowing heart, she said nothing, made no move nor gesture; and yet I knew in my deepest heart that she accepted my daughter, that she would mother Jane for me.

I held my chilly soul up to this hearth-woman, basked in her warmth, and was, for a moment, lifted out of the pit of my despair.

And then she was no longer there, and the timer buzzed the twenty-minute signal, and I got up from the piano bench, and re-entered my everyday world.

But it was no longer exactly the same everyday world. Something had shifted, the tiniest bit, perhaps, but shifted.

Things didn't get miraculously better between Jane and me. This isn't a fairy tale, no matter how it sounds. Things were bad, very bad, and it was a long, long time before they began to heal.

But I never again plunged into the same depth of despair. It was the faintest whisper of hope that the Woman in Black had brought to me, but it was enough.

I never experienced her presence again. Nor did I long for it. What had happened was sufficient.

I *did* wonder, though, and often, who she was. Could she really have been the Virgin Mary? Was she some archetypal goddess or mother-figure? In the end, I never settled on an answer.

Mostly I just thought of her as the Woman in Black.

Sometimes I wondered if she had actually been a woman at all, or if she were Something Else. But what she had brought me, with her enfolding shawl and her glowing heart and her lap to hide in, was comfort, and so that was ultimately the name I invented to describe to myself this sudden, surprising presence that had come to me.

She was the Comforter.

Tuesday's Child

M Y ENCOUNTER WITH AN OTHER at the traffic light so many years before had kindled a spark within me that first manifested itself as restlessness, bursts of activity, strivings. As the years passed, that fire burned into an emptiness that was pure craving, pure because it burned without knowledge, because it was a longing, a hunger, for something whose nature I didn't even know. I craved in ignorance, pure ignorance.

Recently I came across a description by Diogenes Allen in his book, *Temptation,* of the "single, bare, unique desire" to which we must cling "with such attentiveness that we thirst and hunger, yearn and long, for what we cannot even imagine," and this pure, ignorant desire is for God.

If I'd come across that description earlier, maybe I could have made sense of what was happening to me. It might at least have reassured me that I wasn't simply crazy, hunting an invisible, indefinable, ineffable something that had no name, for an unknown purpose.

Searching, looking for love.

I didn't even know for sure it was about God. With all my sophistication and adult studies, my God image still wore a long white beard, had a penis, spoke Hebrew, and inhabited Out There and Up There.

What more was I looking for?

Groping in mist and fog, that's what I was doing. And who could understand, and who could guide?

The manna came from James.

Our friendship went back to my first seminar at Stony Brook in 1974. Our first conversations were all about the nature of poetry and language and literature, but as we came to know one another better, by slow degrees, our conversations expanded in length and breadth and depth. We talked for hours about abstractions like truth and beauty and justice, and then about how they actually unfolded in people's actions, lives, relationships, love and mercy enfleshed in human activity.

And increasingly, we talked about God.

What is the nature of God?

And of humanity created in God's image?

What is the nature of man? Of woman?

For hours.

Whereas in the beginning his conversation was witty, clever, dazzling, delighting my intellect, now it became substantive, deep, inspiring and feeding my hungry soul.

When I first knew James, he and his twin brother John, an artist, were living in a rented house in Stony Brook. After a while they moved much farther away, out to the east end of Long Island. I would visit them there; but it was so far that after dinner with the twins, and staying up until midnight or longer talking with James, I would stay over until morning. It was on one of these overnight visits in 1979 that I had the dream.

It was in the second house they rented, the one with a pool in Bridgehampton, near the pond. There was a small guest bedroom on the first floor; the twins' bedrooms were upstairs. Before I went to sleep I looked across the empty living room and watched the moonlight shining on the small pool beyond. Then I closed the bedroom door, got into the narrow bed, turned out the light, and fell asleep.

And had a dream.

I dreamed that I was in the same small room, wearing my same wine-colored nightgown, but something had suddenly awakened me. It was still dark, and quiet, but I was frightened. I couldn't bear to be alone in that bedroom, with the moonlight so bright outside. My heart was pounding so hard that I could scarcely breathe for the fright. Cautiously I opened the door. The living room was dark and still. I tiptoed across to the stairs, then crept up to the second floor where James was sleeping, and woke him, and told him I was afraid. Please rub my back, I said. So he sat up, and I curled into the warm bed, and James stroked my back until some of the fright drained away. Then, from the edge of the bed James leaned down and kissed me on the lips, not a passionate kiss, but a deep one, and the words that often accompany my dreams, like an emblem or a motto or a comment about them, the words sounded in my head.

The seed is quickened.

And then I woke up in the small dark downstairs room, my whole body filled with an indefinable well-being. I got up out of the bed and went to the door and opened it, to reassure myself that I had never left the room, that this experience, so vivid and so real, actually had been a dream.

The seed is quickened.

In my first waking there echoed a response: This is the kiss of life.

In 1973 I had had the "big dream" of the women in blue who were coming to show me my way. This was six years later; but I knew that this dream was the comment and amplification of that one. I didn't know what this dream meant, but I knew that it was of tremendous significance. It wasn't necessary that I understand it; what had happened in the dream was sufficient.

It was also an embarrassing dream. It embarrassed *me* to think about it myself, and I certainly couldn't tell James about it. I told myself: I've

studied Freud, I've read Jung, I know all about libido and suppressed
eroticism and sexual symbols. So it isn't out of ignorance or denial that
I tell you that the dream was not sexual, as in erotic, sexy. It was sexual
in terms of procreativeness. *Seminal* means the seed, *seminary* comes
from the same root, from semen, it is where new ideas and new soul
and spirit are born.

That's what the dream was about.

James spoke the words to me, the words which quickened within
me, were implanted in my empty womb, where new life began to
grow. The unfamiliar feeling was well-being, and intimations of creativity.

All through 1980 the visits and the conversations continued, their
pace quickening.

God, for James, was a real, objective presence, not a concept of
historical or theoretical interest, nor even an object of abstract belief.
He was a living Being, the Other of us all, the living God who did not
dwell Up There or Out There. In some mysterious way he was present
to us, even within us, quick now, here now, always.

And God's nature, astoundingly enough, was love.

God is Love.

Etched in stone on the Wellesley College Chapel.

Naive, I had thought it. A tempting mirage, wishful Christian
thinking.

Now here was James making the same assertion, that God *is* Love,
nothing less, nothing more. Awesome. But not the punisher, nor even
the rewarder, a Something Else which simply loves its creation, pities
our sufferings and our struggles, gives us help and solace and strength,
not because we earn it, but because to give is God's nature, free-will
offerings, God's gifts to us.

God's grace. That's what James talked about.

November 6, the date of my birth, had been a Tuesday. Do you
remember the old nursery rhyme that begins, Monday's child is fair of
face, Tuesday's child is full of grace, and so on?

I was a Tuesday's child. I accepted my nursery rhyme destiny, that I was to be filled with grace. Of course I thought that meant moving gracefully, meant dancing, dancing through life.

But now, in James's conversations, there appeared a promise of something else.

And what was this mysterious thing that James often spoke of, this *grace?* In Hebrew its quality is elusive, changing according to its context. Sometimes it seems to mean simply God's graciousness, which I always took to mean his good nature. At other times it seems to mean God's mercy, his loving-kindness. But primarily it appears as a statement about God's eternal nature, as one of his attributes. When James spoke about it, however, God's grace seemed to be dynamic, a flowing forth, an *action* which somehow swept up its recipient, gave him or her something needful and beneficial, manna of the spirit for God's children. And sometimes it seemed to be even more, to be a special kind of illumination which, pouring down upon someone, mysteriously transformed and enlightened them.

That was one of the goals in sitting *zazen,* wasn't it? Zen meditation was supposed to lead to *satori,* to enlightenment.

So what *was* this mysterious grace?

James answered my questions as best he could from his own traditional training, thinking, and insight. But I heard his words in my heart, rather than dispassionately and intellectually in my head, because they were too overwhelming.

They only fed my hunger.

How can I find this *grace?*

Tell me.

You don't find grace, James said. Grace finds you.

Because, he said, grace is a gift.

For that matter, he said, everything is a gift, everything we have isn't ours by merit, it is a free-will gift of God. The universe itself is neither necessary or inevitable. It is simply the gracious gift of God, whose nature is to create. And since we don't earn these gifts, we simply receive them, then we can infer another truth about God, that he loves us *as is.* As we are. We do not have to be changed, or finished, or perfected, in order for us to be enfolded in the love of God. Our families, our friends, the rest of the world may love us conditionally, so long as we suit them. But not God. He loves us *as is,* right now. The time is not to come. The time is now.

Did I believe James? I only know that I *chose* to believe him, because what he talked about made sense to me. His was a God worth believing in, true or not, this real and present and loving and mysterious One, this great mystery.

And there was more.

I already knew that God is light—the kindling of the Sabbath candles, light is a symbol of the divine.

Yes, said James. But God is also darkness.

Darkness, and stillness, and silence.

There was even a way of enlightenment that was darkness, a *via negativa* James called it, a mystical way. There were many ways to God, he said, and many people's stories about their ways: Teilhard de Chardin, and Julian of Norwich, Teresa of Avila and John of the Cross and Thomas Merton, Simone Weil and Martin Buber, Gandhi and the Sufis and the Buddha. All kinds of diverse people, because God is not little, but big, and as the father and mother of all people, God chooses us all.

Adon Olam.

Lord of the Universe.

Who is worshipped in particular ways, not because *God* is containable, or needs containing, but because *we* do, because we are incarnate beings, forms of flesh, not disembodied spirits, who therefore need particular rituals and creeds to enable us to worship in our flesh.

Not a popular point of view, James said ruefully.

He said to me once, Have you ever heard of Edith Stein?

She was a Jewish woman, he said, a German Jew who became a nun and died in the gas chamber at Auschwitz, wearing her yellow star of David, a remarkable spiritual woman. I've been praying to her for you, that she will help you find your way, he said, then added quickly, seeing my frown, Not to be a Catholic. That was *her* way. Your way will be your own way. I've been asking her to help you find that way, your *own* way.

I wasn't then very interested in Edith Stein as herself, a German Jewish convert to Catholicism, and a martyr at that, that wasn't my style. What fascinated me was that James was actually praying to someone for me as if that really meant something, as if prayer actually did have consequences.

Such ideas, I suddenly realized, had never even crossed my mind.

And I wondered. All those hours and hours in temple. What on earth had I been doing?

Well, praising God. That's a valid prayer in Judaism, to praise God. And to thank him. But always communally, those prayers were acts of corporate worship recited in prescribed form, integral parts of the holidays in which they are embedded.

I think I had no idea whatsoever of a personal God.

Solitary prayer?

Most shocking of all, he spoke as if it were possible to pray to people as intermediaries to God. And wasn't that what people meant when they claimed that Catholics didn't really worship one God, that they worshipped human beings whom they called saints? They even worshipped statues, which made them idolators.

But James said no. He wasn't talking about worshipping statues, or worshipping saints, for that matter. He was talking about the reality of the communion of saints, he said. The connectedness with all who have gone before is a living reality, he said, and prayer is a way of tapping that energy across the centuries. This is hardly original to James, nor to Christianity: it originates in the Jewish concept of *L'dor vador,* the connections from generation to generation. But whereas the Jewish words were simply that for me, words upon a page, when James spoke of them, they sprang out of flatness into three dimensions, attractive and colorful and alive for me.

Why should this have been so?

Insufficient teaching or understanding? Psychological and temperamental biases? It doesn't matter, really. For whatever reason it simply *was* so. In one form, something was abstract and inert for me; in another, it touched me into life. Not different truths, all a single truth, but I was hearing it through James, and the language in which he was speaking to me was *mamma loshen.*

My mother tongue.

The Yiddish words literally mean "Mommy's tongue," the language of childhood, the first and closest and most intimate of all others, the one that speaks directly to the heart.

How strange that James's language, so philosophical and so Christian, should be the one to touch, not my mind, but my heart.

Hebrew, and Bible stories, and Sabbath afternoon *zimirot* songs, and the Passover seder, the kiddush cup, the twisted challahs, the Sabbath candles, those were all *mamma loshen* to me. But so was all this talk about God's nature and activity that I heard from James.

What else had been *mamma loshen?* A book I read that summer, *The Seven Storey Mountain,* by Thomas Merton. A world unfolded before me in its pages, a world in which, exotic and alien as it was, and without my belonging to it in the slightest, I nonetheless felt *at home.*

There was yet another world I discovered about this time, and that was C. S. Lewis's fantasy world of Narnia, a series of children's books for grown-ups, for the kind of grown-up whose favorite mode of truth, whose mother tongue, as it were, is fantasy and myth.

His Narnia, with its seeking children, enchanted animals, witches, and heroes, appealed to the deepest child in me. His was a world worth seeking, worth leaving *this* world for, as the children did through the magic mirror, to enter another world of beauty, magic, goodness, terror, death, and life beyond life, a world in which love, overcome by evil, rises from its own destruction to a mysterious triumph.

What C. S. Lewis had done with Christianity, I longed to do for Judaism. On the inside back cover of my well-used paperback copy of Gershom Scholem's *On the Kabbalah and Its Symbolism,* I find a list I made in an attempt to begin.

The burning bush is there, and the Shekinah (Veil) and Torah (Scroll), Torah the name, Letters of black fire written on white fire,

Divine Sparks, *Bat Kol,* Pillar of Cloud, Pillar of Fire, Hidden Roots to the Tree of Heaven, the Wine Cup of Elijah and the Appearance of the Prophet, Fiery Chariot, Milk and Honey and Bread, Feast of Leviathan, Banquet of Solomon, The Tetragrammaton.

My own symbols, the ones that were my heritage.

And yet no inspiration came to me from them. Although Scholem wrote sympathetically about mysticism, it was always from the outside: it was clearly understood that such areas in Judaism are regarded with mistrust.

And anyway, I was tired of books.

I wanted *people* to play with, to share these ideas with, more people like James, but Jewish ones, for once; I wanted Jewish intellectual playmates who would speak to me in *mamma loshen.* After all, I was utterly committed to finding whatever I was looking for within Judaism. To leave my own tradition for anything else was literally *unthinkable,* and I never thought of it. So I went looking for such playmates.

And I didn't find any.

Not for lack of looking.

I still went to Tuesday morning adult education study groups at the temple, now being led by the new assistant rabbi, a woman, a very nice woman; but when it came to these amorphous, yet real, ideas I wanted to explore, we made no connection.

I felt lonelier than ever. And frustrated, and confused, and angry.

There's someone I think might be able to help you, James said to me one day. He's a priest.

He saw the look on my face, the distaste, the lifted eyebrows.

Wait, he said. He's an extraordinary person, he's doing amazing things over at Stony Brook. He's very knowledgeable and open, he'll understand what you're doing from a Jewish point of view. But the really important thing about him is that he *connects* people.

Connects people?

He's kind of at the hub of a lot of circles, said James, all kinds of circles, not just Catholic circles. *Through* him people find other people whom they should know. If you want, I'll call him for you.

Reluctantly, I agreed.

But what on earth was I going to say to a priest?

As I stood before the door of an ordinary development house, in an ordinary suburban neighborhood, I was afraid to push the doorbell. Some atavistic sense pushed at me, whispered, Get back in the car and go away. But I had an appointment. So I pushed the bell.

I don't know what I'd expected. Someone dark, handsome, and Satanic? Piercing eyes? A magus? What I got was a middle-aged, middle-sized man with a middling kind of face, ordinary and unmemorable, wearing a rumpled open-collared short-sleeved black shirt, no round white collar, rubbing his eyes and blinking.

Sorry, he said. I was reading and I must have fallen asleep. Come on in.

We walked down the hall to a little room lined from floor to ceiling with books. More books overflowed onto his desk.

So you're a friend of James, he said.

Yes, I said, and began, warily, to talk.

When I emerged an hour and a half later, it was with an indefinable sense of *having been listened to* by someone of high intellect, who didn't find my questions and doubts and desires peculiar in any way. He didn't have any answers for me. People looking for God are on a journey, he said, and the road is rough most of the time, and that's the way it is.

What a relief! I was looking for God, that's all, and I was on a rough road, that's all. Not crazy. Not the only one in the world. One of a whole bunch.

I also emerged with a book he'd given me.

It was the writings of Rabbi Abraham Isaac Kook, first chief rabbi in Israel, who had been a practicing mystic, which was why his writings had been included in a Paulist series called Classics of Western Spirituality. I devoured the introductory biography. Here was someone who'd done it all, the observant and active Jew of the synagogue who was also the solitary seeker after the presence of God. It *was* possible! And how odd that it had been a priest who'd introduced him to me.

But when I turned to Kook's writings themselves, I was disappointed. The images, the symbols, the language, they had nothing to do with me. I found them opaque, unreadable.

I was coming close to giving up the search. Someone suggested I talk to a rabbi, an older man, in Old Westbury. He was a wonderful man, kind, warm, reassuring. And he did seem to understand, *almost*. But not quite. Take another course, study this book, he suggested, or that one. Perhaps that was wise advice.

But it wasn't what I was looking for.

At last I remembered how empathetic Rabbi Joshua Rothstine had been, how he knew a lot about Christianity, and didn't scorn it or dismiss it, he understood its appeal. Perhaps he could help. And so I went to see Joshua.

What is the Jewish equivalent of grace? I asked him.

We talked for a long time, before Joshua said, gently, sympathetically: In the terms you're talking about, there *is* no Jewish equivalent of grace. That's a Christian doctrine, a Christian idea.

And so that was the end of it for me.

I always suspected it wasn't true, anyway. Thomas Merton and C. S. Lewis and my friend James, all deluded. God *isn't* love, and there is no grace.

Once, long ago, God had offered to be with me always, and I had turned him down.

This, then, was the consequence of that refusal, this terrible separation, this loneliness, all the world could understand one another, but there was no *mamma loshen* for me. In November 1980, our son John became a bar mitzvah, and entered as an adult into the covenant of the Jewish people. For better, for worse, I had fulfilled my duty toward my children.

Now, when I came to the temple, it would be for no one's sake but my own.

And I came, to services, board meetings, committee meetings, study groups. I was more active in temple affairs than ever. I still spoke before Jewish audiences. The image was still intact, smashed into a thousand fragments, glued back together again, believer, devout woman, pious Jew. But inside I was different. My hunger, my thirst, all were over. I was Tuesday's child, filled not with grace, but with emptiness.

Discouraged, exhausted, lonely, how was I to know that they were the same thing?

Breaking Open

O NE COLD DANK DECEMBER SUNDAY in 1980, when Frank and I were getting dressed to pay a visit to friends in Connecticut, I said to him, I feel funny. I don't know what it is, I just don't feel well.

Do you want to go? he said.

I don't know, I said. Maybe I'll lie down for a little while.

After half an hour, I got up and began to dress again.

But the "funny" feeling returned, and suddenly I began to gush blood, doubled over with cramping spasms of the worst pain I had ever known, doubled over on the toilet seat, bleeding so hard I was afraid to go to the hospital, afraid I'd bleed to death on the way.

Next morning in the gynecologist's office, I heard what I'd been dreading. Already in 1978 I had bled my way through Israel, and doing research in Washington I had suffered a near-hemorrhage, which perhaps was an influence in my discouragement with my dissertation. It was fibroid tumors that were causing the problem. A dilation and curettage performed a little over a year ago had been nothing better than a stopgap. I had been buying time, because I was frightened of having an operation. Now time had run out. There was no alternative to a hysterectomy.

Do it, I said. Enough pain, enough blood. Get it over with.

Even so, I was shocked later that afternoon when the phone call came from the doctor's office to tell me that I was scheduled to be operated on that Thursday. It turned out to be a blessing in disguise, because I had so many arrangements to make in such a hurry that I had little time for worry or panic, and also because the memory of those agonizing cramps, still sharp and fresh, acted as a powerful incentive. I didn't want to go through *that* anymore.

So on Wednesday afternoon, little suitcase optimistically packed with books, I checked into Long Island Jewish Hospital. Frank was with me, and stayed all afternoon until the end of visiting hours at nine. We didn't talk a whole lot. I had a pleasant roommate, an attractive, smiling woman about my age, who welcomed me cheerfully. Well, why not? *She* was going home tomorrow. Her husband came to see her later, and we all chatted sociably. A little while after that, two monks came to see her. At least I assumed that's what they were. They wore long brown robes, and sandals, and big wooden crosses, which I thought incongruous in Long Island Jewish Hospital, and they held a kind of brief ceremony with her, but I thought it would be rude to look too closely, so I didn't; I politely averted my eyes. I thought it was all kind of pagan. Soon the monks, or whatever they were, left; and after another little while our husbands left, and as the full weight of what was going to happen descended upon me, we began to talk, my roommate and I.

You'll be fine, she said. You'll be just fine.

You can say that, I said. And smiled to show I was just kidding.

I'll pray the rosary for you, she said. That's what my family and friends have been doing for me, so I knew I'd be fine. And I'll pray for you, and you'll be fine too.

I looked over at her. She didn't *look* wild-eyed and crazy, she looked calm and confident. And happy.

I'm Jewish, I said.

So was the Virgin Mary, she answered, and laughed. She was a Jewish mother. She'll take care of you.

Another one. Here was another one like my friend James, who actually acted as if prayer were something real, as if it had real power to effect consequences. What was a rosary anyway? It had to do with beads, like a necklace, and it was about Mary. But how did you pray one? What did you do with it? Wear it? What did you say?

I asked none of those questions, however. Rosaries were for *goyim*. For Christians. But without believing in the thing itself, I still took comfort from her belief, and from her goodwill toward me.

Thank you, I said. I would like that.

She reached out her hand, I stretched out mine, and we touched for a moment. Then the nurse came around with a sleeping pill for me.

In the morning, an injection of Darvon took care of any preoperation nerves. Frank was with me as the gurney rolled from the room through the halls up to the operating-room doors. Then he kissed me good-bye. My gynecologist appeared in his surgeon's greens, and we moved on into the theater: big star on the rolling cart under the bright lights, large supporting cast at the ready. I felt great. I was telling the doctor something important, something really funny as the anesthesiologist began the drip, and in the very midst of the punch line, the lights went out.

I went out.

And then I was back, briefly, in another place, where a nurse talked to me. I answered, and then I was gone again. Whenever I woke it seemed to be dark, and there was pain crouching at the threshold, I'd mumble, and far away I would feel a prick, and I would sleep again. In that fashion a day and a half passed without my presence.

Frank says I moaned and tossed and groaned, but I don't remember anything. We had hired private-duty nurses for the first thirty-six hours, and so no sooner did I wake to pain than I received an injection, and was out again. I'm sure there was a lot of pain, hysterectomies are major abdominal surgery, but I really don't remember anything much except a blur. My first roommate was long since gone. But she'd been right, I was fine, so fine, that on the fifth day there was a shortage of beds and I was, on the recommendation of my doctor, sent home to recover and heal.

That was a long, slow process, and I luxuriated in every bit of it, relished the staying in bed, being pampered, relinquishing chores I didn't much like anyway. No driving, lifting, reaching, carrying, walking up and down stairs. I stayed at home, retired from the world, out of touch with anything but my own body. When I hurt, which was often, and when I was depressed, also often, I would tell myself, that's okay, that's natural, it's part of the process.

St. Francis de Sales put it pithily: Don't be discouraged because you're discouraged.

But I run way ahead of myself, to the time of resurrection. In that wintertime I was in a vastly different place.

It was a long, cold gray January, a bleak landscape. The climax of all my spiritual seeking had resulted in nothing, a barren search by a barren woman. All that the operation had done was to mirror my spiritual condition in my physical self. I was truly a hollow woman.

Through this lonely and frustrating quest for the unknown, my closest companion, of a kind, was T. S. Eliot. His poetry echoed how I was, affirming these feelings of breaking open, of being poured out and emptied.

> We are the hollow men
> We are the stuffed men
> Leaning together
> Headpiece filled with straw. Alas!

The Waste Land, that's where I was, a hollow woman in the vast waste desert land, abandoned, dry, lost, knowing I was lost.

It was a time of waiting, when I still hurt very much, and the staple marks across my lower abdomen were red and raw and painful, when bumping downstairs on my behind and dragging myself back up step by step exhausted me, when day followed unchanging day. Day after day I waited, waited to be healed. And nothing happened. Underneath, my recovery was proceeding slowly and steadily, but it showed itself only in fits and starts. I thought I'd never be comfortable again; then one day I was. I thought I'd never have the energy to hurry up and down stairs; then one day, I was doing it. Seemingly all at once, after unrelenting tiredness, I felt well enough to drive the car. Do the laundry. Shop for groceries. Lift bundles. Return to some activities.

Of necessity I had also had to interrupt my Zen sitting, but I had returned to it as quickly as I could. If God would not speak to me anymore, if no one spoke my language, if there is no grace, then perhaps there is enlightenment, a glimpse of God as Nothingness, as Emptiness. If I cannot have God's presence, perhaps I will have his absence. But the sitting went on, day after day, and nothing happened.

I went on sitting, day after day; and after a while I no longer expected anything, sought anything, hoped for anything. No longer struggling, letting go, I just sat. That's all.

Then my friend James suggested something to me.

I like to use a text as a meditation for sitting, he said. Not to think about, just to read it first, something short, and then hold it within me while I sit. If you want to try that, he said, you might try *Ash Wednesday* by T. S. Eliot. Do you know it?

No, I didn't know that particular poem. But *anything* sounded better than *nothing,* so I took a look at it; and its starkness, its bare, spare, hopeless hoping appealed to me, and I began to read it before my morning sitting, taking the poem (which I didn't understand) chunk by chunk, letting the words resound in my depths.

> Because I do not hope to turn again
> Because I do not hope
> Because I do not hope to turn
> Desiring this man's gift and that man's scope
> I no longer strive to strive towards such things

There I am.
That's it.

> Teach us to care and not to care
> Teach us to sit still.

Doggedly I continued, sitting still, while nothing happened.

The previous fall I had joined an interfaith committee in Syosset. If I couldn't reconcile Christian grace and Jewish teaching, Christian symbols and Jewish concepts, well, then, perhaps I could help to reconcile the actors in this drama, those ancient enemies, Christians and Jews. Many of my dearest friends were Christians, after all. They were hardly my enemies. So I joined the group, and met good people, people of goodwill. But the things they chose to talk about, political and social and behavioral things, to me were beside the point. And no one, of any faith or denomination, seemed to want to talk about faith, or prayer, or God. And when I returned to the interfaith meetings in Syosset in the spring, it all seemed far removed from my own reality. What was all of this? Words, words, more words.

Still nothing happened. Unless I count two crazy notions that began to grow in me. One was a desire for a rosary of my own, not to do anything with, just to have; and it would have to be given to me by someone, not bought by me, nor even asked for, which is *completely* crazy, because who is going to think of giving a Jewish woman a rosary? And the second craziness was that I found myself drawn to the Woman in Black, the Veiled Woman, the presence who had comforted me when I had sat in despair on my piano bench, and to whom I had entrusted my daughter. Not exactly praying to her. It was more a *thinking toward*. She was a memory, and a longing, that's all.

And so I sat. Not waiting. There was nothing for which to wait. No more intellectual speculation. No philosophizing.

Just *do it*.

Just–sitting.

Sitting still, and waiting for nothing to happen.

Alma Mater

*T*HE BACKDROP TO THAT LONG terrible winter of sitting still and waiting for nothing was the final stages of my father's slow and monstrous dying from Alzheimer's Disease.

Alzheimer's is far uglier than words like tragic, or sad, or suffering can begin to convey. It is unspeakable, disgusting, gross, degrading. It robs the brilliant of their intellect, the pleasant of their good nature, the fastidious of their dignity, the self-sufficient of their strength, and all persons of their personhood. It snatches roughly away the entire personality and leaves behind a stranger, an abusive, often violent, incontinent, helpless, ultimately comatose stranger.

Vile. Hateful. And in its beginning, always small.

The first insidious changes are so insignificant they go unnoticed, or if noticed, unremarked upon.

When I was little, I thought my father was better than God. I invested all my love and hope in him. He was mother and father to me. He used to wear wing-tip shoes, and I worshipped the ground he walked on in those wing-tip shoes, bright earth-dwelling angel.

Things deteriorated between us, but he was always my father, powerful, special.

One day at my parents' house I realized with a sudden shock that my jovial, talkative, bombastic father wasn't talking much anymore. He seemed abstracted, withdrawn, and then he wasn't there at all, had left the room, gone to lie down on the sofa.

But quickly I grew used to this lower level of participation. If I thought about it, I suppose I said, He's getting older.

Or hard of hearing. Yes, that was it. In a conversation he'd often ask you to repeat something, or not hear a question spoken right near him. Hard of hearing is a more comfortable thought than—

But in the dining room, if you whispered something to someone else, my father might call out a sharp comment from the den, two rooms away.

Hard of hearing?

The downhill slopes gently at first, almost imperceptibly.

My father is not quite as sharp as he was, not on top of things. Not as curious.

He doesn't bother my mother about the bills anymore. He doesn't bother himself about them, either. There are fewer calls on his office phone, fewer clients coming to the house.

My father was the most fastidious of men, a snappy dresser, meticulously neat.

A spot on the tie?

When was the first time the jacket and trousers were mismatched?

Can that dark stain on my father's trousers possibly be what it appears to be? Not possible. It's possible. It is.

Successive descent over years, each one bringing us to a new plateau where there was time to pause, rest, readjust to lowered levels of performance and expectations.

But then the pace began to accelerate.

My mother coped with my father's memory gaps, with his violent and sudden mood swings, the apathy, anger, irascibility, occasional euphoria. She was shaken the first time her husband called her Mama, but she grew used to it. My father wandered around the house restlessly, but he seemed always to settle down in his bed, and anyway, the house was familiar territory.

But increasing incontinence, in a big house without a bathroom on the ground floor, became too much to cope with. They moved to an apartment, a pleasant, roomy, convenient apartment. My father lost his spatial memory entirely in the move. He would walk from one room to another and stand there, frozen, lost.

We were all now addressed indiscriminately by a jumble of family names, of people alive and dead.

Final descent is rapid.

My father could no longer dress himself. He had difficulty feeding himself, forgot ten minutes after eating that he'd already done so and fretfully or angrily asked my mother where his food was. He needed a cane to walk. The front door had to be kept locked or he would be out and wandering, cane or no cane.

A home health aide came in one day a week, then two days, at the end, six. My father was big and heavy and hard to handle, especially when he was agitated. His temper became increasingly uncertain, sometimes violent. He raised his cane one afternoon to hit my mother.

But the final decision to move him to a nursing home was precipitated by fecal incontinence. My mother finally cried over that, tears of frustration and anxiety and fatigue and rage.

We were lucky enough, at his advanced stage of illness, to get my father into an excellent nursing home within walking distance of the apartment.

But excellent, when it comes to nursing homes, is a relative matter. They are all awful, in human terms, at least my father certainly thought so. We had long known his views about invalidism, and nursing homes, and keeping people alive.

When the time comes, get a gun and shoot me, he'd say. I don't want to live like that.

He went into the nursing home astonished, stunned, betrayed. He "pulled himself together" in the way Alzheimer's victims sometimes can, to meet a sudden crisis or stimulation. But very quickly he went into a deep depression and refused to eat.

They tied his hands, and inserted a feeding tube.

Frantically we protested.

He's just depressed, we can't let him starve, they said.

Of course he's depressed. He wants to die, he's ready to die, he doesn't want to live like this.

When the time comes, get a gun and shoot me.

We could hear him speaking through now-silent lips.

I don't want to live like that.

It wasn't so easy.

His fever spiked. He went to the hospital. He had pneumonia. They began antibiotics. The feeding tube was still in place. His hands were still tied.

Desperate, I went to see my acquaintance the priest at University Hospital.

It's inhuman! What can I do?

Coached by him, I tried an appeal to the Ethics Committee. And lost. The psychiatrist's diagnosis of depression induced by admission to the nursing home, therefore temporary, therefore reversible, was upheld.

The feeding tube remained, the antibiotics dripped into his vein.

There is only one memory I care to retain from those dark days, and that is when my father lay in the hospital bed in a coma, and I sat beside him, looking at him, not really thinking, just sitting, and after a long time, I picked up his hand and I held it. My father always had beautiful hands. I'd grasped them tight as a child, watched them trace the outlines of Hebrew words for me, draw funny faces on eggs, his shapely hands.

And only now, with him in a coma, could I once again hold his hand and let the love flow freely between us, the love that had been blocked for the greater part of my life.

Comas are mysterious things. Later, much later, I used to wonder, and then hope, and finally pray, that wherever *he* was, not his body that lay on the bed, but the essence that was my father, that he knew, that he felt, at last, the love and respect he'd always wanted.

Early in May 1981, the day after the Ethics Committee in its wisdom decreed that he *must* live, my father died.

Aspiration pneumonia, the death certificate read, a common consequence of feeding tubes.

They insisted on saving him, and probably killed him instead.

Me, I think my father's spirit wandered off from that unmoving body in the bed, attended the Ethics Committee hearing on his own behalf, returned, looked with pity and compassion on its earthly home, and simply decided not to return.

They couldn't beat him in the end.

There was a big funeral, and at the cemetery, his sons-in-law and male nephews and cousins each took the shovel to scatter clods of earth on the coffin as a final honor and service, but his daughters, who wanted to do so, were not permitted by the rabbi.

My father's long dying was complete.

The month of formal mourning ended in mid-June, at the time of the twenty-fifth reunion of the Wellesley College Class of 1956. My old roommate and I had spoken about it, hesitant, ambivalent. In the end it came down to this: I will if you will.

Twenty-five years.

Wellesley's daughters had been eager young women rushing toward the wide wide world. Now, in our mid-forties, we would be returning to our alma mater, bearing the weight of a quarter of a century's living, returning to discover—

Who we were? Who we are? Not me. I was done with all that.

I set out on that June Friday in the same spirit as I had sat every day for so long now. It would be nice to see my roommate again. Otherwise, I expected nothing, sought nothing, hoped for nothing. What the weekend would be, it would be; and that's what I was going to encounter, not myself. Something other than me. Not-me.

Because what was there left of me, anyway?

I went to my twenty-fifth reunion wide open, back to Wellesley, my alma mater.

The word *alma* descends from the Latin *almus*. Used of a nurse or of a breast, it means life-giving, nurturing, fostering; as an epithet of female goddesses or priestesses, it means kindly, gracious. It is from this double sense of a cherishing, nourishing, fostering mother that we come to call our university, college, or school our alma mater.

Alma has other meanings as well. The most familiar is a feminine proper name. In Italian, the word means spirit, or soul, which is how Spenser used it in *The Faerie Queene,* the personified soul, *Alma.* Hence, we could justifiably claim *alma mater* as our "soul mother," the mother who brings one's spirit, rather than one's body, to life.

I never was a gung-ho Wellesley girl. More often during my four years there I felt like an outsider than a daughter of the house. I've kept in touch with no one. Why am I going?

What do I expect to find?

Myself?

At least I knew the answer to *that* question. The young woman who spent four years among Wellesley's "tow'rs and woods and lake" exists nowhere now, neither among the living nor the dead. I came with no illusions about reliving an idyllic past. I doubted how idyllic it actually had been; and, in any event, the past cannot be relived. The title of Proust's epic, *À la Recherche du Temps Perdu,* is generally translated as *Remembrance of Things Past.* But the French means literally, the "Search for Time Lost." Perhaps that was it. I wanted to find what had been lost without my even recognizing it, what I had lived without even knowing it. To look upon the past, uninvolved, detached, all passion spent, at last to encounter the truth of the past.

Or perhaps it was just plain curiosity.

What do my classmates look like now, a quarter of a century later? (Better than me?)

What have they accomplished? (More than me?)

I realized that I was letting myself in for a heavy dose of "alumnae magazine syndrome," the depression occasioned by reading class notes in the quarterly issues of the alumnae magazine, in which everyone else's children are simultaneously attending Harvard, Yale, and Princeton; their husbands are billionaire entrepreneurs or ambassadors or prizewinning research scientists. The syndrome is a common one, but it's especially virulent in the pages of Wellesley's alumnae magazine; and the ensuing depression can last for hours or even, in bad patches, days. And here I was, venturing into the lion's jaws of direct contact with these superwomen.

Why am I doing this?

At least I was fortified by the knowledge that I had had a book published, however disappointing its sales, and I made sure to tuck a copy in my suitcase as a talisman.

I unpacked the few things I'd brought and wandered downstairs, eyeing these well-groomed, well-dressed matrons who had once been my classmates. I didn't recognize anybody; but that's why God invented name tags, isn't it? Squeals began to echo through the entrance hall.

I can't be-leeeve it!

And what do we say after, I don't be-leeeve it! And the other exchanges, soon exhausted, by which we define ourselves: our old nicknames, our marriages, our divorces, our children, our jobs or lack thereof. What else is there to talk about?

Supper that evening was cafeteria-style. Waiting in the hall, waiting on line, sitting at supper, I found the most interesting woman to be one with whom I had scarcely exchanged two words when we had been students; and the other interesting women I met were those who had experienced divorce or deep failure of some kind. They had a wisdom, a humility, and a patient acceptance that was at the opposite pole from the arrogant entitlement of alumnae magazine class notes. Something had happened to these misfortunate golden girls to transform them into real people, and they came alive for me.

When my former roommate arrived after supper, and we went to her room to talk, there was an initial awkward reacquaintance, and then I discovered with relief and delight that she too had become a real person, alive and vivid; it was a joy to be with her.

Saturday evening's banquet reenacted old-time "school spirit." It was an occasion of insider allusions and self-congratulations to which I had always been an outsider, and I felt familiarly restless, uncomfortable, and forlorn; until I realized with an uncertain shock that the sensation which I was labeling *forlorn* might just as easily be called boredom, because I was *bored* with these things, bored with the invocation of the past except insofar as it was involved and implicated in the present.

Who are we? How did we get this way? How did we get from *there* to *here?* Those are the things I wanted to know, the questions I cared about, not, Do you remember? and, Wasn't it great when we—

The banquet was boring.

Sunday was the day of class parades, white dresses, class hats and adornments, assorted banners and emblems and regalia, hundreds of alumnae marching.

But I did not choose to march, did not want to dissemble an alien heart under a mask of smiling unity. I would wander the campus by myself, revisit the towers and woods and lake, those inanimate things that in the long run were what was still most alive about Wellesley for me, the living spirit of place, her *genius;* and for which so far this crowded weekend there had been no time.

And so I set out alone on my way. Not lonely, for once. Simply alone. It was a beautiful June day, and the campus was radiant. The sun shone on me, my heart shone within me, quietly, peacefully, happy just to be here among the greens and golds, the blue of lake and sky, just to wander undisturbed.

On the path leading toward the library, I encountered Meg, another refugee from the parade.

Meg had been in my freshman dorm, a dry, laconic Vermonter, who had then moved all the way across campus so that, for the next three years, we had probably never even had a conversation. Yet I remembered her with warm affection far beyond our actual en- counters. Meg had always touched my heart. Together, the two of us, we wandered the quiet, peaceful campus.

But Meg's heart was neither quiet nor peaceful. It was disturbed and heavy. A career sacrificed to her husband's, lies and betrayal, an ugly divorce, financial problems, a declining father, a teenage daughter to support and contend with. Meg that day was far from any kind of smiling unity. But she knew well enough why she had come to the reunion.

We stood by the lake behind the library. Her words emerged slowly from the silence.

I was in the depths, she said, after the divorce. No money. No job. Everything was terrible, there was no hope, I couldn't see any way of getting out from under. I felt like nothing, cast off, unwanted, just *nothing*. I felt like I didn't belong anywhere, she said. My daughter was away. I had this tiny apartment I was renting, but it certainly wasn't home. *Home* was where we'd all been together, in Washington.

We stood watching the ripples on the shore.

One day I was out driving, she said, and I discovered I was near the campus. I thought to myself, Maybe they'd let me use the library. Maybe if I tell them I once went here, maybe they'd let me use it just for a few hours or something, even if I don't have a card, or proof, or anything. So I drove onto campus and parked and went down to the library and I thought, I once went here. This beautiful place, I once belonged here. It didn't seem real, she said. I didn't belong anywhere anymore. I walked in anyway. But I didn't know what I was going to do if they turned me away. There wasn't any farther down to go.

I introduced myself to the woman at the desk, Meg said, but before I even got around to explaining, she smiled and said, Welcome! How nice to have you come back to us. You don't need a card to belong here, the woman said to me. You already belong. How can I help you?

It sounds melodramatic, what Meg said next. But it wasn't. It was just a quiet statement of fact.

Wellesley saved my life, she said. I belonged somewhere. That was enough. I could pick myself up and keep on going.

A canoe put out, almost noiselessly, from the boathouse. I don't know whether Meg was crying or not. I watched the canoe. After a little while we walked on along the path as it curved around the shore, then began to climb the hill beyond. We walked in silence mostly. Every now and then a few words would bubble up between us and fade away. Companionably we began to climb the steep flight of stairs that departed from the lake path and ascended the back of Tower Hill toward the cluster of Gothic buildings up above.

On a mutual impulse we stopped halfway up the steep stone stairs. We turned around to face the lake. The sun was still high in the sky. Four ancient Greek columns slightly below us were framed against the blue, transported from somewhere to form this idyllic Classical vista, columns, lake, sky, sun, pines. We just stood there, absorbing it. Then we began again, in silence, to climb the stairs. They were so steep that our first view of the back of the Tower complex was on a level with our heads, a ground-level view, not so much a walking-toward as an emerging-up-into. A few steps more, and we were on the same level, and there it was. How can I explain to you in words, which are linear and consecutive, something which was a single image complete in the moment, a sudden presence perceived whole and entire in an instant of time: three buildings of gray, ivy-covered stone, a central building and one on either side, strong arms stretching toward the lake, and a grassy courtyard, *hortus conclusus,* a garden enclosed, green lawn cut by a quadriform path, and at its heart, where the paths intersected at the center of the cross, flowers spilled over from a stone urn, a riot of flowers. That was what was there, what I saw in the instant. But what I experienced then was not an inanimate landscape, but life, a living presence, Alma Mater, soul mother, whose arms of stone reached out to me, whose grassy bosom waited to embrace, who drew me in.

Welcome! breathed the stones and the grass and the ivy.

Welcome! This is where you belong, just by being here. You don't have to earn this, and it can never be taken away from you, or lost. You are Wellesley's daughter, the same as all her daughters, and this is your home, this is your place, this is your mother, you can rest now.

It is already accomplished.

*L*ech *L*echa

I DROVE BACK DOWN FROM WELLESLEY to Roslyn happy, although that is perhaps too active a word. Satisfied. Content. At peace, safe harbor reached, home free all, and strangely, quietly exalted, because it was accomplished—what was lost and never known is found—there is nothing left to do. It is already done.

The search is finished.

And yet, on Monday morning, when the hour came round at which I was used to sitting, I went over to the piano bench and I sat.

Not *for* anything, because that was done, over with, nothing more to hope for or to dread. And yet I sat anyway, just-sitting, *shikan taza,* for no reason, companioned still in the blank silence by poetry, the final words of Eliot's *Ash Wednesday* coming alive within me:

> Blessed sister, holy mother, spirit of the fountain,
>   spirit of the garden,
> Suffer us not to mock ourselves with falsehood

Teach us to care and not to care
Teach us to sit still
Even among those rocks
Our peace in His will
And even among these rocks
Sister, mother
And spirit of the river, spirit of the sea,
Suffer me not to be separated
And let my cry come unto Thee.

A week I had of it, a week of calm finality and certitude. Twenty minutes every morning on the piano bench, for no particular reason. Life was ordinary again. I was at rest.

A week.

And the following Monday morning, I was sitting again, expecting nothing, light, innocent, when something happened. I had thought nothing else was going to happen, but I was wrong.

Something terrible happened.

God spoke to me.

Seven years it had been, seven years since God had kindly offered to end my loneliness with his presence, and I had, in terror, refused. Seven years to repent of that refusal, seven years to give up any hope of hearing God's voice again. It is truly said, Be careful what you pray for, because you will get it.

So now God spoke again to me, and it was terrible; because this was no kindly, gentle, loving offer of companionship. This was the voice of command, of He-Who-Must-Be-Obeyed, the stern, compelling voice that Abraham had heard, with the same message, in Hebrew, I heard it.

Lech lecha.

Get up and go out.

Again it came.

Lech lecha.

Oh my God!

The voice sounded within me, but it was not my voice. It was an Other's.

And then my response, sounding within me, uttered without speech, wail of despair: I always knew it would come to this!

O my people, what have I done unto thee?

I was knocked off the piano bench, blasted to the floor, annihilated, all physical sensations; and yet I never moved. I sat there on the piano bench frozen, heart stopped, the end of the world, the end of my world.

Get up and go out.

As feeling returned, the tears came, gushed forth, I put my hands over my face, rocked back and forth, wild sobs, the kind of sobs that were only a vague memory from childhood, racking ugly sounds, so undignified! I sat there rocking, grieving, for days, hours, minutes, until the sobs at last subsided, and still I sat, desolate.

There was no question of a refusal.

This was no offer. This was a command. And I had already said yes, upon the instant, before any thought, before I had decided my decision was made, and I had consented, I had answered, Yes.

Yes, I said.

I had no choice.

If, as Diogenes Allen suggests, the reality of an encounter with the divine is the "initial unattractiveness of its terms," which always involve renunciation, this was surely an authentic encounter with divine Reality.

I was devastated.

Get up and go out.

Go where?

I had no idea, no understanding of what the command meant in practical terms. And yet I knew immediately that it meant what it said, it meant leaving, renouncing everything that was my own, my people, my tradition, my history and identity, because those things, my people and my tradition, they *were* my identity.

O my people, what have I done unto thee?

And now, having been obedient, having agreed to leave, now what was I supposed to do?

What happened next was not based on rational, logical, sequential thinking. I did not decide on a course of action and proceed, step by step, toward a chosen goal.

The opposite.

When the sobbing had died down, and my voice was under enough control for me to speak again, I went to the telephone and my fingers dialed the number of the priest at the University Hospital at Stony Brook. He would know what this extraordinary and unwelcome phenomenon was all about. But when I asked him, Do you have time to see me today? he replied, No, I don't.

Oh, I said. Now what was I to do?

He must have heard something in my voice, because he said, If something is really the matter, I guess I could—*Is* something wrong?

Yes, I said. Then, No, I said.

I don't know, I said.

And then the words came out of my mouth, not from my brain, from somewhere else; I only heard them in their strangeness after I said them, this conversation is one I listen to as if I am not involved, as if I am eavesdropping.

Do you say Mass at the hospital tomorrow? I heard that strange "I" saying.

Yes, he answered.

May I come, I said.

Of course.

What do I have to do?

You don't have to do anything, he said. Just come to the chapel, it's right in the lobby, ask at the desk, and come in and sit down, that's all. Mass is at noon, so come a little before.

Oh, I said.

Can you tell me what this is all about? he said.

No, not till after the Mass tomorrow. If I come.

You mean I have to wait until then?

Yes, I said, and hung up.

Why shouldn't he have to wait? I had to wait as well, I had no idea what I was doing, or why, or what would happen, or what this was all about.

All afternoon tears flowed, ebbed and flowed again. I was sick at my heart. That evening and night were terrible. I had to greet Frank, be with the kids, serve supper, business as usual, smile, stem the tears that welled up repeatedly. I couldn't tell anyone. What could I say? Oh, by the way, God spoke to me, he said *Lech lecha;* and how was *your* day?

I lay awake most of that night, dreading the next day, on the verge of refusing the command, knowing that it was already too late.

I was mostly numb Tuesday morning as I drove along the parkway toward Stony Brook.

What am I doing here?

No, God, I don't want to do this.

I parked the car, and walked into the hospital lobby, my heart pounding. I asked for the chapel, received directions, walked over to the door, reached for the doorknob.

And all the fears and emotions and memories and stories which had been lurking just behind me, glimpsed out of the corner of my eye, took sudden shape as Furies, screeched and swirled around me, attacked in force.

You are going to the *goyim.* You can't go to the *goyim.* They drink, they all drink, they call Jews Christ-killers, they call them that so they are free to kill Jews, these are the drunken Jew-killers, the Holocaust, the gas ovens, all of it, all behind this door, lampshades made of Jewish flesh, here they are, pogroms, murder, rape, torture, Cossacks on their rearing stallions, Jewish blood runs in the streets, knives, machine guns.

THIS IS THE PLACE OF YOUR ENEMIES

Auto-da-fés, Jews in dunce caps bound and set aflame to illuminate dark Spanish nights.

BLOOD ENEMIES

Don't touch that knob!

These people worship *statues*. We Jews bow the head and bend the knee before *no* man, we are a proud people, a Chosen People.

They soar and swoop, my Furies, fear, hatred, pride, howling at me.

Take away your hand, you are going over to the enemy, you are deserting us, you are going over to death, you will be destroyed.

Another voice. An unknown voice.

Behold, I set before you this day, life and death, good and evil. Therefore choose life, that you may live.

Who is saying that? Which way is life? Which way death? Enter? Or leave?

I closed my eyes. I felt faint. How could I go through with this, how could I stretch forth my hand?

O my people

How could I not? I had come so far, I could not turn back. Could I? Once before I had refused. This time I *would not* turn back.

In fear and trembling, not knowing what pagan monstrousness lay beyond, I took hold of the knob, pushed open the door, entered the chapel, closed the door behind me, and found—

Not very much.

A small quiet room, so dark I had to wait for my eyes to adjust to the twilight. Several fat candles burning, a small bunch of flowers, a wood panel picture leaning against the wall, fitfully illumined by a flickering candle before it. I had been afraid of what would be on the wall, distorted Jesuses on a cross, dripping blood or something. But there was nothing on the walls except a quite beautiful abstract painting in three panels, sky colors, blue and sunrise and sunset. The room was empty and very still. I sat down on a hassock, my back firmly to the wall, and waited.

A few people came in, sat down or knelt on the floor. And then my acquaintance entered, but now he was a priest for sure, wearing a plain white robe, a stranger to me. He entered swiftly, noiselessly, and knelt down on the floor, facing the people.

Silence.

Then he said, The Lord be with you.

And people replied, And also with you.

How strange it all was, how unfamiliar, how alien. I was almost afraid to look.

And then I heard the priest say, O house of Jacob, come, let us walk in the light of the Lord.

Well, I knew *that*. That was *Jewish*. What was going on here?

Someone read something that was really familiar to me, I knew it, of course, it was from *my* Bible. Not theirs. My tense muscles relaxed a little. I began to listen. Really listen.

The priest lifted a plate and blessed bread, or so he said. I couldn't see what was in the plate.

Blessed be God forever, he said.

He lifted a cup and blessed the wine, fruit of the vine, he said.

I knew that, too. Oh, did I know those gestures, those words! Every Friday night for most of the years of my life I had seen my father raise and bless the bread, the wine, offer it to us.

Eat. *Ha-motzi lechem min ha-aretz,* the challah, bread from the earth.

Drink. *Boray p're hagafen,* the kiddush cup, fruit of the vine.

The priest, my father, the same.

This ceremony, rite, whatever it was, was very quiet. So was the flow of words the priest was saying in his flat, unemotional voice. And so, the things that I really heard ring clear in my ears seemed to emerge from silence, and withdraw back into silence.

In him we live and move and have our being, he said.

Let us offer one another the sign of peace, he said.

And there were handshakes, kisses, embraces. I pressed further back against the wall. I greeted no one, touched no one. But I watched.

The plate upraised, This is my body—

The cup. This is my blood—

The priest knelt on the floor, and the flickering candles cast his shadow behind him, darker than the dark walls. But then it was as if the shadow was *not* his, the shadow was itself a presence, arms upraised, even when the priest's were not—a presence offering me the plate, speaking through the priest's lips, a shadow I dared not name by name, for the very name of Jesus is anathema to the lips of many Jews, and I among them; so this shadow who offered me the bread was simply He in whose Unnameable Name all this was being celebrated; and he offered me the bread, he offered me the wine, mine for the taking, stretch out your hand.

Taste and see the goodness of the Lord.

And something else I heard, everyone together said, Lamb of God, you take away the sins of the world, have mercy on us.

Have mercy on us.

Grant us peace.

Yes, please.

And the priest held up a round white wafer, and I heard the people say, Lord, I am not worthy to receive you, but only say the word and I shall be healed.

Oh!

So words can heal, a word can take away sin, and heal the wounds left behind, and here are the words, these words, a balm around my heart, an indescribable healing bath, peace bathing my inmost self.

And at that moment it was as if bandages, invisible bandages that had bound me like mummy wrappings, suddenly burst, and fell away, and left me exposed, my unhealed wounds all raw and bloody and oozing, wounds that had been neatly hidden away under tightly woven bandages that I had thought were my everyday clothing, my chosen garments. But I was alive now, real now, and here I sat, in a hospital, all unhealed, but free to the air, free to breathe, hearing a promise of healing, an unimaginable promise.

The priest passed from one to the other, offering the bread, offering the wine, and I sat and gazed, as the Israelites must have gazed on the Promised Land, desiring these things with all my being. This is what I want, this bread, this wine, this is my hunger, this is my thirst, this peace, these are the words, this is *mamma loshen,* this is my mother tongue; here, where I have never been before, here is what I recognize, here is my own country.

I have come home.

I gazed, and I desired, my wonder and attention like a child's, and like a child, I simply wanted this celebration to go on forever.

But it didn't.

There was total silence for a little while, a blessed silence, and then the priest made a sign, said some words.

Go in peace, he said, and it was over.

I was not in peace, I was in a turmoil as I left the chapel. I have no idea what I said to fill in the minutes of small talk with the priest, who had remetamorphosed into my acquaintance, in the hall, in the elevator with him, entering his office.

And then the small talk stopped.

Well, he said. What did you want to see me for? What's all this about?

With shock, with horror, with inevitability, I heard the words emerge from my mouth at the same time he did, with no intention, no choosing, no decision, simply my self responding to my own necessity, I heard my own words.

I want to be a Catholic, I said.

And let my cry come unto Thee.

What Happened Next?

*T*HAT WAS NOT, OF COURSE, the end of the story.

It was the beginning of the rest of my life, but it certainly felt at the time like the end of everything.

To my surprise, and if I am honest, to my chagrin, my acquaintance the priest did not rush to gather the lamb into the Catholic fold. Evidently there was a whole process of discernment that came first, a testing of the spirit, it might be called.

Where did this impulse come from? Was it caprice? Boredom? Instability? Neurosis? (Not that neurosis and God are unacquainted. Far from it.)

I had assumed Catholics were only too eager to convert Jews. I was wrong. It was almost nine months of testing and study and struggle before that momentous Easter Sunday when I was baptized, confirmed, and received first Communion.

Nine long months. Difficult for me, at least as difficult for my husband.

Appropriately enough, it was on a Tuesday that Tuesday's child had attended that first fateful Mass. It was Saturday before I worked up sufficient courage to attempt to explain to Frank what I was going to do.

Come for a walk, I said. I have something I want to tell you.

I cannot remember ever having been more nervous in my life, perhaps not even when I turned the doorknob to enter the hospital chapel at Stony Brook. We walked for a while in silence. I couldn't find words to begin. At last I blurted out something.

I've been praying to the Virgin Mary.

Oh? said Frank.

Yes, I said.

More silence.

Finally I said flatly, I want to become a Catholic.

Frank stopped, then turned toward me.

Thank God! he said, and put his hands on my shoulders. I thought you wanted a divorce.

I leaned toward him, babbled in relief. No, of course not, no—

But the relief was short-lived. I tried to explain what had been happening to me, but since I didn't understand it myself, it was hardly surprising that I made a poor, incoherent job of it.

Meanwhile, what I was proposing to do began to sink in.

Frank's first response was a joke: If you're going to do something wild like become a Christian, at least be an Episcopalian. They have more class, he said.

But then he began to hear my seriousness, and I in turn heard his growing unhappiness and hostility. Frank had never cared for ritual observance, for temple services, the things which, unconsciously, I equated with Jewish identity; so I assumed, I suppose, that he wouldn't care very much about this change. I was wrong. He cared a lot. He cared, not about the rules, but about the Jewish people, their history and persecution and struggle to survive. He was proud of being a Jew. Observance had nothing to do with his feelings.

I felt worse and worse, increasingly guilty and increasingly frightened.

We've been married for twenty-one years, he said. And we're very happy, we have a good marriage. This is going to change things. Do you really want to do that?

My heart had already sunk as low as it could. From somewhere I mustered a response of courage I was far from feeling.

Yes, it will, I said. But it could change things for the better, couldn't it?

It's already better, he said, frowning. All I can see is worse.

I hope not, I half-whispered. I loved this man, but in these moments I was afraid of him. I wanted to do this thing more than— But I also wanted my marriage, and my life as it was.

Choose—

And as if reading my thoughts, Frank said to me, What would you say if I asked you not to do this? For me?

Terrible words.

I walked a little farther, then began, I don't know, I'd have to think—

He interrupted.

I wouldn't ask you to do that, though, because even if you agreed to give it up, I'd lose. You'd always feel you'd given up something important to you just because of me, I would have forced you. If it's that important, I suppose you better do it, and we'll have to take our chances.

His face was as grim as his tone.

Guilt flooded me, but I was aware that mingled with the guilt was relief. This desire of my heart was possible, at least for now.

A wise man, a generous man.

An unhappy man.

He would have nothing to do with my acquaintance the priest, whom he blamed for enticing me. The anger had to go somewhere, after all.

The process of becoming a Catholic was arduous. I cried more tears than I thought my body contained, experienced anguish and tearing apart. The only peace or joy I could count on was attending the

Eucharist, which brought its own tears, but I experienced them as healing. I went to the hospital chapel for Eucharist during the week. For a long time I was too raw and vulnerable to go to a local parish church, or any Sunday celebration. Sunday is a family day, and I was separated now from my family, not in fact, but in spirit. I was lonely even in the tiny, intimate chapel, set apart from my fellow Jews, not a Catholic. I felt as alone as anyone in the world. Often the only solace I felt, the only understanding, came from an awareness of the presence of Jesus the Jew, a marginal person like me. If no one else knew or understood, he did. When everyone else rose to receive the wafer that I learned was called a host, and I sat alone, I felt him sitting with me.

And I could not, dared not, unburden my heart to Frank, who, I was sure, would urge me to leave this ill-framed venture and come back where I belonged.

But I didn't belong there any more. I didn't belong anywhere.

I don't know how matters would have turned out if not for a few extraordinary people whom we encountered then.

There is an ecumenical community named Taizé after the little town in Burgundy in France, where it was founded in 1940 by a Swiss theology student, Roger Schutz, who had come to Burgundy to shelter Jewish refugees from occupied France. After the war, he, with a few fellow Protestants, established a small community in Taizé, inspired by the monastic tradition.

During the worldwide student unrest of the 1960s, Taizé was suddenly overrun by thousands of young Europeans seeking—something. They themselves didn't know what. But they were drawn to Taizé, attended the liturgy, soaked up the silence. Brother Roger and the other monks welcomed their unexpected visitors—so many, from so many different places—and felt the need to simplify and reshape their liturgy to accommodate the diversity.

By the time I heard about it, Taizé was long established in France as a unique ecumenical community. Their distinctive prayer features one or two lines of text, often in Latin, chanted again and again in simple melodious lines. And candles, icons, flowers. And silence.

Silence is at the heart of their worship.

I had first heard of this community from my friend James, and I had been intrigued. Now I discovered that there were actually a few Taizé brothers living on Long Island, and people were welcome to come and pray with them.

My appetite for prayer seemed insatiable then. I called and asked if I could come.

Of course.

So I did, and discovered the silence. It was balm to my heart. There is no controversy in silence, no dispute or dogma or doctrine, not even any history.

Sitting together, in silence.

How was it? asked Frank.

We were warily friendly these days.

Okay, I said. I think I'll go back next week.

When I prepared to set out, though, Frank said, I'm coming with you.

I suppose I looked as stunned as I felt.

If that's all right, he said hastily.

Why was he coming? I wasn't so sure it *was* all right with me. Did I want to share this special haven? Would Frank spoil it for me?

What's it like? he said.

Oh, I don't know. There's a lot of silence.

I like silence, he said.

And he did. Sitting on the floor in the dim room, sitting in silence punctuated only by the fewest of words, reinforced by the simple repetitive chants, he told me later, he had for the first time ever felt *at home* in prayer.

And with the brothers, who asked us to stay for tea.

The third time I went, I went alone, and had to leave immediately after because the brothers had a private meeting. The fourth time, Frank came with me, and again we were invited to tea. I was not perhaps *actively* jealous, but my nose was a little out of joint. Clearly Frank was more interesting than me! (The persistence of character flaws through even a profound spiritual experience is perhaps reassuring.)

Brother Yan, a Dutch psychologist, and Frank seemed to establish a special rapport. We began to go regularly to pray with the brothers, then have tea and conversation.

Frank found solace that at least some Christian company was compatible. He, who had no interest in theology, at least none that I ever knew of, suddenly engaged in long conversations with Brother Yan, without embarrassment, even eagerly. These conversations were not about Christianity or about Judaism.

They were about *God*.

Of course you believe in God, Brother Yan said to Frank. You believe in a cosmic God, that's all. The others are too small for you.

Oh, said Frank. Of course.

So simply did he take his own first step on his own spiritual quest, his own—not mine, not anyone else's.

And thus that challenge to our marriage that we had been so afraid of began its movement toward the better, and has grown and flourished until the shared life we live is full beyond all our expectations.

What happened?

Frank remains Jewish. He has no desire to be anything else, nor would I wish him to be. He often jokes, I'm the only person I know who'd been married twenty-one years and suddenly had a mixed marriage; but our mix is not oil and water, incompatible. It is our own unique blend, a blend of me, and him, and both-of-us, the things we can share and the things we cannot, but which we regard with respect and reverence.

And our children?

When I finally gave myself permission to live my life as my heart dictated, I found the capacity to grant that same privilege to my children. And when expectations are removed, so too are much of the disappointment and disapproval that so often poison families. My children watched me choose a path uniquely—and strangely—my own, and somehow they absorbed that they could choose paths of their own also. The issue here is, as it always truly was, *freedom,* to choose, grow, experiment, even to fail, without the burden of further failing to live up to someone else's blueprint of a successful, worthy life. I had never before had the courage either to take, or to give, such freedom. Only then, emboldened by God, did I begin.

Both children are well along the way of becoming the people they are. As for religion, they left that to their mother when she was Jewish, and continue to do so now that she is Catholic: it's *my* thing, not theirs, they say. And they're right.

The mission of the brothers of Taizé is reconciliation, so it is hardly surprising that their influence upon our lives has been reconciliation.

Reconciliation in our family.

Reconciliation, in our marriage, between Christianity and Judaism.

And reconciliation in our friendships—which have expanded to extend beyond the borders of this country all the way to the places of my childhood enemies, who now have new shapes, new faces. Three German women in Cologne and in Erbach have become the dearest of sisters to me, as is the Japanese woman with whose family I traveled for five weeks through Japan as *obachan,* "auntie," living in the homes of people whose culture and aesthetics I always loved, but who, like Christians, were enemies to me by history and by inculcation.

Not that history doesn't exist, or doesn't count. But we can live beyond history, beyond the categories, if we are prepared to take certain risks.

To dare to change—

To dare to try—

To dare to trust—

Not the fruit of action, but the *action* of action.

Zen precept—Just DO it.

A new beginning, still unfolding. And, if I am brave enough to keep on trusting God and following his motion in my heart, it will keep on unfolding even unto death.

And beyond.

Afterword: Forgive Us Our Trespasses

T IS ENOUGH YEARS LATER that I begin to have some understanding of the meaning of my experiences, what I call experiential theology.

Sometimes I cannot believe how lucky I am. And that is true, not
only of the good things, but of the bad. Before I was frozen, numb,
insulated, dead; now I have become living flesh and blood, so that I
can *feel* things, pain and pleasure. I rejoice more, I suffer more.

I am alive.

That is what my experience of healing has been, coming back to
life. Not instant healing. I don't believe in such a thing. Healing, if it is
to be real and permanent, is a long and slow and generally painful
process. What happened to me at that first Eucharist was the *promise* of
healing, and the promise began the process, which eventually gave me
the courage to enter a long course of psychotherapy, which I have
found to be my way to truth, that is to say, to reality.

Truth. Reality. Those are only other names for God, two of the
faces which God wears, to allow us to know him by.

But then it follows that seeking to see and to know the truth is as terrible a quest as to see and to know the face of God, because they are the same. From where do we get the courage for such a quest?

My courage came in my experience of that first Eucharist. The central thing that I experienced that day in the twilight of the hospital chapel was not communion.

It was forgiveness.

That is the heart of the matter, that is the central action of this supreme sacrament, the first thing, in fact, that happens in the ritual. We repent, and we are forgiven.

> Kindness and truth shall meet;
> justice and peace shall kiss.

That is what the Psalmist sings, and what is enacted in the Eucharist.

The importance of that Eucharist for me was not the offer of bread and wine. I was familiar already with those things. It was the moment when the mummy wrappings burst, when I was set free, the moment when that which was lost was found.

Here it was, the moment of grace, the grace for which I had so long sought, God's unconditional love and forgiveness.

The movement with which we reach for God, says my friend the priest, is the same movement with which God reaches for us. A moment initiated by God, but mutual nonetheless.

Mutuality, the perfect circle, the Nothing which is Everything is achieved in penance and absolution, and consummated and celebrated in communion. The sacrament of reconciliation is the painful recognition of yet another failure, the relief of naming it, and the joy of the love that says, Go and try again, my child, my beloved. One single movement, a circle, the reconciliation of God and his creation, which is every one of us, believer, nonbeliever, every color, every race, every tongue under our star-sun, and beyond, to the ends, if there are any, of the universes. The music of the spheres is a song of forgiveness.

I *know,* because I had lived my life until then, I suddenly realized, in a world without forgiveness, in a world where, even if there were God, he was remote, powerless or indifferent to forgive and save. And therefore everything depended on me, mistakes were permanent, and therefore fatal; and my father's perfectionism and my mother's superstitions were the wisdom of such a world, an attempt to safeguard themselves and their children from the terrors of this kind of world.

A terrible world.

A world of despair. And that is why despair is the ultimate sin, *despero,* to lose hope. To be hopeless is to deny God's power to change things, to heal what is essential in us, our deepest, unique selves.

In a world of a faraway or indifferent God, in a world without forgiveness, how is it possible to look upon the truth? Who can bear it? We are not perfect (nor are we meant to be, although we don't realize that), and therefore we make mistakes. Repeatedly. And, to guard ourselves from those terrible failures, many of us choose denial. Mistakes are inadmissible. It is the only way we can survive; and so we live in a state of sinfulness.

Sin is an unfashionable word these days. Even in the centuries of its popularity I suspect it was misunderstood.

Most of us are actually pretty good people, and are trying to become better people, so why do we need forgiveness so much anyway?

The New Catholic Encyclopedia defines *original sin* this way: "a condition of guilt, weakness, or debility found in human beings . . . prior to their own free option for good or evil. A state of being, not an act or its consequence."

It takes a lot even to be *capable* of deliberate sin, grown-up sin, sins of free will. The truth is that many of us are so unaware, so caught up in denial and compulsions and defensiveness, that we can only live in this quasi-innocent state that is original sin. We live prior to our "own free option for good or evil" because we are *not* free, adult, responsible persons. We are, many of us, profoundly *unfree,* children, slumbering or half-awake, or, like Sleeping Beauty, in a twilight trance of enchantment. We have not even the capacity to choose good or to choose evil.

Sin is, first of all, an inheritance: "The sins of the fathers shall be visited upon the children unto the third and fourth generation," says the commandment.

And that's optimistic.

The chain of blindness, of compulsion, continues a lot longer than that, is handed down endlessly, *l'dor vador,* from generation to generation. We inherit our sins, pass them on to our children, and they to theirs; and all of this we do in the most profound ignorance. Our childhoods are contaminated as were those of our parents', and their parents before them, back and back and back. We are involved and participate in this ignorant sin, and the world around us, with its wars, addiction, pollution, exploitation, testifies to this truth. But it is not our intention, there are no personal villains; but all are victims, receivers and dispensers of the inheritance, unless, at some point, the chain is broken.

Forgiveness is the weapon that permits us to open our eyes and see through our veil of protective lies.

Your sins are forgiven, said Jesus to the paralyzed man. Take up your pallet, and walk.

But sin is also misunderstood in its more conscious dimension, those sins that we are, to whatever degree, capable of choosing and committing freely. We are inheritors, in our Western world, of the Greek tradition, which portrays sin as *hubris,* willful and arrogant action. To that extent sin can appear to us glamorous, bold, defiant, sneakily admired. But there are very few great sinners in that manner among us. Far more of us are guilty of what Kierkegaard accurately described as sins of impotence and passivity. He links sin less to active assertion than to the Christian tradition of sin as despair, and specifically to the despair of "not willing to be oneself."

In that form, the abdication of authority and responsibility, and the refusal to will to be oneself, sin is common to us all. But it is especially endemic among women, because it is a sin that masquerades as virtue, and it is encouraged by the society in which we live.

Sin, then, is not wicked actions nearly so much as it is the mummy wrappings, the ones that burst open for me during the Eucharist in the hospital chapel, the bonds that imprison our true selves, and prevent us from showing our original faces.

Show me your original face, the face you had before your father and your mother were born.

I had been guilty of the sin of refusing to be myself, and I had been guilty also of the sin of refusing God's forgiveness. Because what else was the meaning of that experience of the *Bat Kol,* the daughter of the voice, who spoke to me at the traffic light in 1974? God offered his company, and I refused it because I felt unworthy, and was frightened. I condemned myself. Not God condemning me. *I* did it. God forgave. I could not forgive myself. Sometimes I think that is why it took seven years, and the necessity for me to pass from one tradition to another, for me to be free. If I had been able to answer yes in the first place, would I have become a Catholic?

I doubt it.

But I wasn't able, and I said no, and the story went on, not another way, but *this* way, the story I have told to the best of my ability, and as truthfully as I know how.

And now I suffer a little from "teller's remorse."

These events have been the most private, most hidden, most mysterious of my life. To hold them up to public gaze is difficult enough. But when they form a narrative of dreams, visions, voices, shadows, then embarrassment is added to remorse.

Do you find such things strange? Irrational? Naive? Embarrassing? So do I.

I am not a person who *believes* in such things. I have no interest in Lourdes, am skeptical of Fatima, would never even have considered going as a pilgrim to Medjugorje. I am a woman of intellect. An elitist.

It is mortifying to admit that my own spiritual quest has been as mystical and experiential and emotional as any peasant woman's.

It's mortifying. But it's funny, also, with a kind of poetic justice: how the mighty are humbled. Or black comedy.

The other part of teller's remorse is that I expose my own ignorance and uncertainty. Do I *know* that I have been following God's will?

Know, for instance, that *Lech lecha* meant go to the Eucharist, become a Catholic? Of course I don't know that.

I can only look back over my recent life and assess: have I grown or diminished? Become more, or less, responsible? Loving? Charitable? Compassionate?

I can know only those fruits which have come to maturity, and only partially know those; and so, like everybody else, I go forward in fog and uncertainty, day by day, right foot, left foot, doing the best I can. Trying to intend the best. Trying to follow the truth.

But *knowing?* For sure?

No.

And really, if I could, where would be the adventure?

What else is living, but doing just that, going on, day by day, right foot, left foot, journeying? Now I journey in hope. That's the difference.

Robert Louis Stevenson said it best: To travel hopefully is better than to arrive.

And that's the point, isn't it?

Why do I tell my story anyway? The story of an ordinary woman leading an ordinary private life?

It's valuable because it is *my* life. It is unique. It is my own shape. No one since the beginning of the world has ever lived out my destiny, and no one, until the end of time, will ever live out my destiny again.

I am unique, a unique event, a *singularity* in the universe.

That uniqueness is my birthright as a child of God, and an image of God.

And it is everyone's. It is yours, and yours, and yours, whether or not you believe, it doesn't matter. You are a son of God, you are a daughter of God, created in God's image, and your history and your destiny belong only to you, unique, irreplaceable.

You are a singularity.

Never again will there be a you.

Then how can we doubt our own value?

Without each of our existences the world would be diminished by precisely that particularity which belongs to us alone.

Not a sparrow falls, but it is marked.

And why should I expect to rest?

There is no rest for any of us until we are once again reunited with *Adon Olam,* the Lord of the Universe, that Phenomenon, Him/Her/That in whom we live and move and have our being. Our story does not end until we do, until we pass, not from one tradition to another, but from one existence to the next.

You have formed us for yourself, O God, and our hearts will never rest until we rest in you.

Not fare well, then, but fare forward, voyager.

Onward.